THE FILIGREE CROSS

The Salvation of Larry Broadfellow

By

Marlene Baird

This book is a work of fiction. Places, events, and situations in this story are purely fictional. Any resemblance to actual persons, living or dead, is coincidental.

© 2002 by Marlene Baird. All rights reserved.

No part of this book may be reproduced, stored in a retrieval system, or transmitted by any means, electronic, mechanical, photocopying, recording, or otherwise, without written permission from the author.

ISBN: 1-4033-6376-5 (e-book)
ISBN: 1-4033-6377-3 (Paperback)

This book is printed on acid free paper.

1stBooks - rev. 12/18/02

Dedication

To my family with love,

*And in memory of five dear friends
who departed too soon*

Irene, Carol, Nita B., Nita H. and Arloa

PROLOGUE

IN 1948 Reverend Patrick Brannigan and his bride, Gillian, arrived at Trinity Church in Chicago eager to embrace Patrick's first congregation. Typically, their day began with breakfast as the sky lightened, the meal timed to coincide with delivery of the morning paper. Within a few months they learned that sharing toast and coffee would provide their only private time until well after the sun had set.

Patrick spread the paper open, covering the table setting that had served a dozen ministers before him. Leggy blue herons pranced around the edges of the milky plates—a design Patrick felt inappropriate for a clergyman's table. He would have preferred no embellishment at all; nothing should compete with whatever God had provided for a meal.

Patrick scanned a report of a devastating apartment house fire which included several photographs. His eyes locked onto a picture of a young boy. Fear had stretched the youngster's face into a flat mask. He appeared mesmerized by the flames reflected in his bulging eyes. Straight, skinny legs poked out of underwear, and his arms hung by his sides with the palms turned outward.

"Gillie, look at this poor young boy," he said. "I've never seen such a look of hopelessness."

Gillian left off pouring the coffee to peer over his shoulder. "Dear God, he couldn't be more than five or six." Resting a hand on her husband's back, she read the article.

"This fire was only a few miles from the church," she said. "His family might be among our parishioners." In one movement she peeled off her apron and grabbed up her purse. "I need to find out who this boy is."

PART ONE

1998

The Letter

Marlene Baird

CHAPTER ONE

IN HIS DRESSING ROOM BACKSTAGE, Larry Broadfellow stripped off his sweaty shirt. He bundled it and rubbed his upper body with the drier parts, then tossed it onto a chair. The wardrobe person would pick up his laundry, including the suit. Everything he wore had to be washed or dry-cleaned after each performance.

He was accustomed to the smell of perspiration, but tonight it was laced with a pungent, acrid odor cause by nerves. It had been a pitiful performance.

Just as he stepped out of his slacks, a knock sounded at his door. He pulled them back up. "Yes?"

"Mr. Broadfellow? Mr. McLaren wants to see you."

Larry mumbled "no doubt," then secured his waist button and opened the door part way. It was one of the many men who ran the cameras and lights. They came and went and Larry never mastered most of their names.

"Where is Mark?"

"There's a small room just down the hall." The young man pointed. "The door has a number four on it."

Larry drew a cotton knit shirt over his head and exchanged his pants for pleated khakis. Mark McLaren was the church's public relations manager and the last person he wanted to see. His lousy performance had been judged by someone less forgiving and far more vocal than God, and Mark had his own ten commandments. Tonight Larry had broken number one: *Thou shalt not, under any circumstances, lose your concentration when in front of the camera.*

To give himself another minute's reprieve, Larry left the dressing room and stood at the edge of the stage. He watched the last of the three thousand who had attended the service straggle through the exits of Gammage Auditorium. He hadn't sensed any disappointment among the audience; perhaps they had not noticed his transgressions. But, then, they forgave him anything so long as they left the service sheathed in sufficient armor to hold temptation at bay for a while.

Larry moved down the hall and opened the door numbered four. He stepped inside surprised to see Jimmy Makaani, the church's leading tenor, there. The room was barely large enough for the three men, a couple of folding chairs and a TV monitor on a table.

McLaren was waiting, poised. The moment their eyes met he started. "Larry, for God's sake, I've told you a thousand times, you never know when the camera is going to be on you. Look at this." He clicked the remote with a perfectly groomed thumbnail, and there Larry stood, eyes squeezed closed and his head

The Filigree Cross

bent as if in prayer, while he adjusted and readjusted the set of his coat jacket. McLaren rewound for a second and showed it again.

Larry marveled that his sins could have been captured so perfectly, then repeated before his eyes so soon after having been committed. The very technology on which the church's success depended had turned on him.

"It's clear you're not concentrating on prayer when you're fussing with your damned coat," McLaren said. "And what about all those hesitations? Sounded like you didn't know what the hell you were going to say next."

Mark had never claimed to be a devout man, but the cursing sparked Larry. He poked a finger in Mark's direction. "You get out there in that mad crowd and try to do better. So I lost my train of thought for a second. No one noticed. I *had* them." He held up his hand and grabbed a fistful of air. "Right here. And I'll have them tomorrow night, and next week in Albuquerque, and next month and next year. So get off my back."

"The only thing bigger than your paycheck is your damned ego, Larry. It's going to do you in if you don't pay attention."

Larry bit back a retort which would have made Mark's language seem pale. There was just enough truth in what the man was saying that Larry simply outstared Mark, then sank into one of the chairs.

Unfazed, Mark turned to Jimmy Makaani. "And you—" He clicked on the tape again, freezing a frame. In a cruel close-up the Hawaiian was shown standing next to Larry with his facial features twisted into a fierce scowl. "What's that?" Mark sneered. "It looks like you're in mortal pain. If that's the way you pray, or cry, for God's sake just stand there with a straight face and close your eyes."

Makaani ran a handkerchief over his forehead and it came away wet. "So tell the cameramen to be more selective. Anyway, Mark, you wouldn't know a real emotion if it struck you in the heart. Larry's right. You're never out there. You should try it some time. People crying and shouting. It's a madhouse."

A knock on the door cut off Mark's reply. Gerry "Tech" Swanson opened the door half way and stuck his head in. The nickname Tech, shortened from Technicolor, derived from the small man's wardrobe. He favored lime green shirts, bright suspenders, and patterned socks—a gaudy flower among the dark suits of the ministry. As always, he grinned and greeted them with typical irreverence. "Hi, ladies," he said.

"What's the news from the finance department?" Larry asked, glad of the interruption.

"I just talked to Chicago," Tech said. "The phones are going ballistic. A hundred and twenty thousand on credit cards alone, the first half hour. We'll go well over a quarter mil tonight. Don't you just *love* the desert." He ducked back out.

Larry glanced at McLaren, who had lost his steam.

Jimmy Makaani clapped McLaren on the back. "Gosh, Mark, I guess they didn't notice my fake mortal pain," he said.

THE GLEAMING BLACK LIMO GLIDED into Phoenix traffic, curious onlookers unaware it carried one of the most recognized religious figures on earth. Larry sank gratefully into the cold leather seat.

The Filigree Cross

The soothing quiet inside the car helped to dissipate his aggravation with McLaren. Though Mark could be a real s.o.b., he knew his job. Public perception, Mark would rightly say, paid the bills.

Larry tried to recall exactly when performing had become such hard work. He could cast his mind back over twenty effortless years encompassing thousands of television broadcasts and live services. He had always been rock solid. He had never groped for his next thought, drawing almost unconsciously on a vast storehouse of words and phrases that fed him as effortlessly as grain sliding from a silo. Tonight, even the microphone had felt foreign. He'd been aware of the dangling cord, the bulky mesh bubble against his lips, the grids on the rubber grip. He could feel them now. Stupid. He rubbed his right palm vigorously on his thigh then scrubbed at his face with both hands. Perhaps he had simply said the words too many times—repeat anything often enough and it loses its meaning.

He concentrated on the inconsequential details of the darkening streets: an angry cabby giving the finger, pedestrians bunched on a corner anxious for the signal to change. He saw a couple running arm-in-arm. The woman grinned up at the man as their bodies jostled one another. Clearly, they inhabited that special world of the carefree, newly-loved, a world beyond Larry's experience. These were the hours of promise—the end of the day and the beginning of evening—and Larry would rather face midnight alone. He and Fiona had never owned this magic time, and yet he had lived it a thousand times. He often imagined coming home to her in a warm kitchen, or meeting her at a diner. He saw them sitting at a gaudily lit window, their joy spilling into the night. He closed his eyes against the brilliance of it, and when they reopened, he was alone in the hard-bought privacy of the limo.

Among the women who rushed along the street, he saw a few who reminded him of past romances. But no one ever reminded him of Fiona. She remained unique—as lovely as Venus in the morning sky and equally remote.

Fiona's mother, Gillian Brannigan, however, touched him every day of his life. If Fiona was bluebells and crocuses on a prairie, Gillian was the crusted earth that split open to bear them, and he loved one as much as the other. And if doctors were to be believed, Gillian was dying.

The limo turned off Camelback Road and slipped along the elegantly landscaped driveway that curved to the entrance of the Phoenician Resort. Here a massive underground water system fed the desert intravenously, producing spectacular results. Larry saw angled spotlights that would light the undersides of palm fronds and broad-leafed shrubbery after dark.

"Will you need me before the service tomorrow, Mr. Broadfellow?" the driver asked as he parked.

"No. One-thirty will be good. Thanks."

LARRY UNDRESSED AND PULLED ON the hotel's robe. His shower would have to wait until after the call to check on Gillian. But before he could dial, the phone rang.

"Larry? Mark here. Look, I—"

"Forget it. You're right. It was a lousy performance. I'm overtired."

The Filigree Cross

"I'd had a hell of a time earlier. The extra security detail we were promised didn't show so we had to bring in some odd-balls at the last minute. Made me nervous. We wouldn't have these kinds of problems if Sue were here. You'll be talking to her; let her know how much we miss her."

"I will," Larry said.

"How's Gillian doing?"

"I'm about to find out."

Larry dialed the Brannigan mansion in Chicago, picturing Reverend Patrick Brannigan, the church's founder, sitting in his favorite green chair, fingering one of his dozen Bibles. Patrick wore out the corners on a leather cover every six months just caressing it. A stroke had left one cheek paralyzed; Patrick's face pulled awkwardly when he spoke, and when tired, he slurred his words. Tonight, beneath Patrick's struggle to be understood, Larry heard deep pain.

"Larry? Thanks for calling. How's Phoenix?"

Larry decided on a kind lie. "The service went well. But we needed you out there tonight; everyone missed hearing your message."

"I owe you so much, carrying on without me again."

Larry recited the words that Patrick expected. "The Lord was with me, as always."

Larry hesitated, reluctant to address the subject that was uppermost on both their minds. After a moment's silence he realized that Patrick would not instigate it. "How's Gillian?" he asked.

"She's failing. You may have to cancel Albuquerque next week."

"Surely she's not that bad."

The old man's voice cracked. "She's so brave. I haven't heard a word of complaint. The doctor said it won't be long."

Larry didn't believe Gillian could have deteriorated so rapidly. She had beaten incredible odds many times. As Patrick's young wife she had faced scandal, poverty and crippling grief. She had devoted her entire life to Patrick and his church, asking nothing for herself. Now, in her seventy-ninth year, God had seen fit to inflict upon her a cancer advanced beyond treatment. Larry regularly preached that solace could be found by trusting in the Lord's wisdom. His own words rang in his head, utterly meaningless.

"I'll be back tomorrow night, right after the service. Tell Gillian I need to see her."

"Don't expect too much."

Surely Patrick was exaggerating; Gillian would smile and take his hand and they'd talk, like a thousand times before. Needing to hear better news than this, Larry asked, "Patrick, is Sue there?"

"She's been sitting with Gillie. Shall I get her?"

"I want to tell her how much the whole crew has missed her."

Larry heard the receiver bump the table as Patrick put it down. Patrick and Gillian had raised their granddaughter, Sue, as their own child since infancy. She had become a lodestone for the church family, exuding a quiet strength far beyond her twenty-six years. Larry had intended to tell Sue of the production problems they'd encountered on this road trip because of her absence, but the moment he heard her voice he realized that the outside world would be of no interest.

The Filigree Cross

"Oh, Larry, I don't know how we'll manage without Grandma."

Larry's heart jumped. So Patrick was not being an alarmist; it was that bad.

"And poor Grandpa. If this doesn't do him in—"

"You just take care of yourself. Patrick will survive. Patrick is tougher than either of us, and he has his God."

"We *all* have God, Larry." It came out quickly, chastising him. Larry had never heard that tone of voice from Sue before, and assumed fatigue had drained her. She finished more softly. "What we need is courage."

"You know, if I could, I'd cancel tomorrow's service."

"Grandpa wouldn't want that."

"Well, you get some rest. Do you have a nurse, some help?"

"Yes. I'll let her take over for a while."

"I'm coming home right after tomorrow's service to help in any way I can. Will you tell Gillian I need to talk to her?"

"Larry, she hardly talks."

He couldn't listen to any more. "Just tell her. She'll understand."

LARRY SLEPT FITFULLY. HE CALLED Chicago several times during the next morning but the reports about Gillian didn't change.

Backstage that afternoon he straightened his shoulders and stretched his neck. He took deep breaths, trying to draw an extra burst of energy from his tired body. Other problems aside, the second time in any city was a little tougher than the first. It seemed that the more eager audience came the first day so subsequent performances required more energy to elicit responses. Also, the congregants were more hesitant to open their wallets for "Love Offerings," or to buy the ministry's books and tapes. Occasionally the facility would not be sold out, though that was not a worry this time since Gammage Auditorium was smaller than many of the venues they used.

Larry spread the curtain a few inches and scanned the auditorium. The lights dimmed, then the sudden burst of the choir's voices stunned the crowd. From experience Larry knew every person in the audience sat awestruck, swept up by the magnificent music which swirled around them in the darkness.

As the choir finished in a climax of Amens, Larry felt the familiar rush of blood coursing in his legs. His skin soaked up the electricity in the air, setting his hands to tingling. Grateful for the adrenalin, he opened the buttons on his jacket and strode onto the stage to a tumultuous welcome. People scrambled to their feet, clapping and shouting.

He leaned into the standing mike, hands upraised. "Thank you for coming," he shouted over the cheering. "Thank you for coming to God's service."

He plucked the mike from the stand and ranged the stage, flicking the trailing cord. The microphone fit comfortably into his hand; it had lost the strangeness of yesterday.

Relieved, he called, "We've got *good* news today! *Great* news!"

Hallelujahs and Amens rose above the general clamor. He swept one arm wide, toward the heavy curtains as the crowd began to settle. "We've got salvation waiting, right here in the wings. Just behind those curtains. We could flip them open. Shall we? Just flip them open and let salvation flood out?" That set some people chuckling, and he laughed along with them.

Then he stopped at the edge of the stage and asked, "What if it *were* that easy?" He waited while the audience quieted.

"What if we could just come to a service, say the right prayers, make a few promises, and flip open the curtain? Think about it. So easy."

He walked a few steps, raising his eyes to encompass those in the upper levels. "What have you ever accomplished in life that easily that you appreciated for more than a few minutes?" He let the question hover in the air for a moment, then continued with a lowered voice. "When a child shows compassion for others, that is a parent's great accomplishment. Did it come easily? Or was raising that child full of challenges, even heartsickness?

"We know that salvation requires similar dedication and selflessness. And we want it to be difficult to attain, for then we will cherish it and appreciate it for the rest of our lives. To accomplish this, certain burdensome things are required of us. Generosity, forgiveness, sacrifice—the list is long."

When he stopped speaking he could hear his listeners—thousands of them—breathing. He knew they'd come for an easy, entertaining way to salvation. When he made it sound tough, they backed off. But a rhythm was necessary: the leading, the falling away, the hope, the disappointment, and then the success.

Preaching was an intricate dance, and he reveled in his mastery of it.

He played on the audience, eliciting responses, ensuring their attention was riveted to his every movement and word. He took them on a journey of hopefulness where they could see themselves becoming better people.

Forty-five minutes later, by the time he had them truly examining themselves, he was dripping with sweat. He surrendered the stage to Jimmy Makaani, who led the choir in a hymn.

Larry showered and changed to a clean, matching, suit. The second time on stage, at the end of the service, he would be easier on them. They expected to be sent home happy.

CHAPTER TWO

JOHNNY CAMERON GROANED and rolled over in his rumpled bed, wrapping the pillow hard around his ears. Taxi horns, sirens, and sunlight had intermittently disturbed his heavy sleep, but what fully roused him was the music of the religious channel creeping down the hallway from the living room. It set his teeth on edge. His grandmother would be watching that evangelist and singing and praying under her breath for the next hour or more.

Johnny kicked at the sheets, venting some of his frustration and slipped his legs into jeans that held their own shape. Cold air drifted through the window opening, raising goosebumps on his bare arms. The sleet and snow of Minneapolis would soon erase from memory this summer of his senior year. He stumbled along the hallway toward the kitchen, rubbing sleep from his eyes.

Then the nightmare came back to him. He grunted at its foolishness. He had been bound by cables to the counter of the convenience store. His fair hair had thinned to spidery wisps, his scrawny frame permanently bent. It was easily interpreted. For weeks he had been receiving rejections from colleges where he had made scholarship applications. Every day the mail confirmed that the sprawling campus of his fantasies would forever remain a dream.

He grimaced as his bare feet encountered grit on the kitchen floor. It was way past time to mop. He flicked open the cupboard and pulled down the economy-sized jar of peanut butter, wondering where the fairness was. This line of thinking was futile, he knew, but last night he'd had no help closing up, and he'd mopped so much junk off the floors at the Kash 'N Karry that his bucket of water was black.

The theme music for the Church of God's Love faded and the choir belted out a hymn. Johnny reached into the bread box, then cursed. He'd forgotten to bring home a loaf of bread.

He absently screwed and unscrewed the greasy, fat lid of the peanut butter jar, thinking about his grandmother in the next room. For at least a dozen years she had been sending money she couldn't afford to the television church. She idolized its evangelist, Larry Broadfellow. As far as Johnny could tell, her sacrifices had not done her one bit of good. After all this time what on earth did she expect? That God might suddenly notice she was in a wheelchair? That He might cure her diabetes and bless her with good eyesight again?

Suddenly she called from the living room, her voice straining over the sounds from the TV. "You have a good sleep, Johnny?"

"Sure, Gram," he shouted back. "Where are they broadcasting from today?"

"This is from Phoenix."

The Filigree Cross

Johnny wondered about winters in the desert.

Suddenly her voice became shrill with excitement. "I think I saw it, Johnny! On the screen . . . my own letter, I think I saw it. It had a pansy border like that writing pad your Aunt Jessie gave me."

"It wasn't your letter, Gram," he shouted back at her. "Trust me." He had opened that letter when she asked him to mail it on Friday. He'd stuffed the fifteen dollars in his pocket and tossed the note and envelope into the dumpster behind the store. Now, remembering, he dug deep into his jeans pocket, retrieved the wadded-up bills and put them into the topless brown jug that held their grocery money. But he could have let her believe it.

Johnny moved across the grimy floor and slouched against the doorjamb, looking into the living room. Leaning forward in 'Bessie,' the name his grandmother had given her wheelchair, she scrutinized the television screen. The camera panned a long table strewn with thousands of letters. Some were in hurried, scratched handwriting, some neat inside computer-generated margins. Many were on fancy stationery, their contents framed by gilded scrolls. Johnny sighed. Regardless of their form, they were misguided, desperate pleas. Just like Gram's.

The camera lingered on a close-up of the letters then swung over to the speaker. The evangelist's voice rose and fell, as ceaseless as the wash of the ocean, repeating the same old message. Johnny guessed it helped to be handsome, and Broadfellow was that. He was in his middle fifties, tall and slim, with just a hint of American Indian in his face. Johnny noted the perfectly cut suit. What would it have cost? Five hundred bucks? A thousand? Maybe Gram's contributions for the past year had bought a sleeve.

Johnny watched Broadfellow lower his head over the clutched microphone, his free hand raised high. The evangelist squinted as if looking inward for inspiration. His brow furrowed in apparent concentration.

"Hallelujah, the Lord hears us. The Lord hears us. If you have written today about your upcoming operation, be assured He will be with you and help you through it. If you've written about . . ." The preacher hesitated, pressing stiff fingers to his forehead. His eyes turned upward, then back to the table before him. "Uh . . . about . . . perhaps you're having money problems and you've written about a bankruptcy. The Lord will send guidance to see your problems solved." Then, suddenly, as if he were anxious to end it, he swept his arm in an arc above the table, shouting, "Hallelujah, Jesus. We love You."

A soaring chorus of voices and instruments rose beneath his incantation. Then the music hushed and Broadfellow dropped his voice to a confidential tone. "Dear God. You are answering us today. We feel You here in this wonderful auditorium. We feel You reaching out to the thousands watching from home. We know You hear us."

Johnny smirked as he watched the evangelist pull his lapels, then adjust the way the jacket sat on his shoulders. He enjoyed the show of discomfort.

The camera pulled back, sweeping across the entire audience. The telephone number and post office box address that appeared on the screen were large enough

The Filigree Cross

for even Johnny's grandmother to read. But, then, she had them memorized.

    Johnny watched her lean back in her chair, crossing her wrists over her chest. She closed her eyes and a peaceful smile played on her lips. He shook his head and walked down the hall to the back porch where they kept the mop and pail.

CHAPTER THREE

WORRIED ABOUT GILLIAN, Larry had not been able to rest on the flight to Chicago. Just eight days ago she had held his hand and laughed with him; now she was near death. These last weeks, maybe months, must have been incredibly difficult for her, but she had hidden her fears and pain.

As his cab approached the Brannigan mansion Larry saw, through thickly-greened branches, that there was a light in the living room and one upstairs—a glow from the room he knew to be Gillian's. Among the gracious residences in this reclusive neighborhood, the home's sandstone and marble elegance commanded attention. Gillian Brannigan had influenced every aspect of the design and it reflected her strength and grace.

Larry unlocked the massive front door and it swung silently open. The crystal chandelier in the foyer, usually blazing, hung in shadow. A uniformed nurse emerged from the living room, apprehension on her face. When she recognized him, relief softened her tired features. She reached to shake his hand. "I'm

The Filigree Cross

Mrs. Daley, the night nurse. Patrick is asleep and Sue is with her grandmother now."

Gillian's room was warm and stuffy, smelling of talc, lotion and something medicinal. In the meager glow of a miniature Tiffany lamp, Larry could see a shallow mound where Gillian lay beneath the covers. Her granddaughter slept, curled up in a massive chair.

Larry nudged Sue gently on the shoulder. She raised her eyes to his, then rose quickly, taking him in a desperate hug. They rocked back and forth as hot tears soaked through the front of his shirt. He led her from the room and closed the door behind them.

"I'm sorry you've been alone with this. I should have canceled tonight."

Sue shook her head. She retrieved a tissue from the sleeve of her sweater and tidied up her face. The weave of the fabric on the chair was pressed into her cheek and her brown hair was mashed flat. Wide dark eyes, always easy to read, drooped with sorrow.

"It's happened so fast. Even since your last call she's changed dramatically. The doctor said her organs are shutting down one after another." Her thin lips quivered. "When Grandpa visited about an hour ago he nearly fainted."

"You get some sleep. I'll sit with her, and I'll let you know if there's any change. What do I need to know about medications?"

"She's not able to take pills anymore. She's on an automatic morphine drip. The doctor assured us that she's comfortable." Suddenly Sue gripped his sleeve and her face contorted like a child's. "Larry, she can't even do something as simple as swallow." She buried her face in her hands and Larry hugged her again, shuddering himself as the enormity of it began to sink in.

"What can I do for her?"

Sue wiped at her eyes and brought herself under control. "The doctor suggests that we keep talking to her. About anything and everything. He feels she can hear, even if she can't respond."

Sue stood on tip-toe and kissed Larry's cheek. "I'm so glad you're here."

She moved, heavily, toward her room. Larry saw that the back of her skirt was rumpled and baggy as if she'd been in it for days.

He reopened Gillian's door and entered quietly, hesitating at the foot of the bed.

"Gillian, do you hear me?" he asked. "It's Larry."

She didn't move.

When he walked around the bed and snapped on a second lamp, his heart skipped. Her skin was waxy white. Flattened lips stretched around an open mouth and the lids of her closed eyes seemed translucent. Cheekbones threatened to poke through tissue-like skin.

She took a long, raspy breath and pushed it out again. Larry counted a few seconds of silence. Then there was another breath, shallow, like an afterthought.

Larry fell to his knees and put his head against the mattress. "Oh, my God, oh my God," he intoned, wishing with all his heart that he could believe God was available to them. He reached under the comforter and found her arm. He gently stroked the fragile skin with his thumb.

"Gillian, it's Larry," he whispered into her ear.

The Filigree Cross

Her eyelids quivered, the muscles around her eyes tensed, and she looked upward.

"Larry?"

The word was as soft as a sigh; if it hadn't been his own name Larry wouldn't have recognized it. He rose to his feet and leaned over her. Their eyes met.

Gently, he traced the fine line of one eyebrow. She responded with the slightest pull at the side of her mouth.

"Gillian, what can I do for you? Please tell me."

"Water," she whispered.

Larry examined the bedside table and found no glass. There was a bowl of water and a stick with a sponge on the end. He soaked the sponge and dabbed it across her lips, then he squeezed the end, allowing a few drops to fall into her mouth.

"Per-fect." The word came shakily, clearly drawn from the last of her resources. She sucked at the air. "I waited for you."

He sat close to the bed, holding her hand and couldn't speak.

Suddenly Gillian's whole body trembled. Larry lurched forward. "Are you in pain?" he asked.

"It's nothing." But her chest rose feebly. "Larry—"

"Don't talk. Let me talk. Let me tell you about the Phoenix trip."

"Larry, I'm sorry." Her lips didn't move; the words slid out of the narrow opening. He leaned closer to hear. "Sorry about the letter."

He was about to ask what letter she meant, but now her eyes lost their focus and gazed upward. He gripped her hand. "Gillian, I love you, Gillian. I don't think I ever said it aloud, but, surely, you always knew."

"I'm afraid."

Oh, God. Oh, God. Larry began to panic. This was no time for an easy answer. She needed honest guidance. How to help her as she'd always helped him? His mind groveled among practiced platitudes, searching for something real, but his tongue failed him.

"Gillian, don't be afraid," he said.

She seemed to sink even further into her pillow. Larry realized he was holding his own breath, waiting for her next one. Finally hers came, shaky and hoarse. After a few moments her eyes closed and her breathing eased to a halting rhythm. He traced her lips with the wet sponge again and put a few drops of water in her mouth, but got no response. He sat back in his chair, hating himself for his failure to ease her fear as she had done for him, so long ago.

HE WAS FIVE YEARS OLD. He awakened in his bed coughing and choking, opening his eyes to searing heat that made him blink. A hissing sheet of flame climbed the opposite bedroom wall. He leaped from his bed and ran for the doorway, screaming for his mother but yellow rubber arms held him back. He kicked and squirmed to be free but the monster hauled him to the window, then dropped him. Breathless falling. Hands and arms again, a rough blanket against his cheek, screaming sirens.

For a long time he was unable to recall those details—it seemed as though he'd been born on the church steps, dressed in someone else's clothes and holding the hand of a pretty woman who became Gillian.

The Filigree Cross

He'd had a mother and father and a baby brother, too, before the fire. But there were no pictures, no toys that he'd played with. He hadn't started school yet, so his young life was lived within two square blocks of his home. Since the fire had razed the adjacent buildings, nothing remained even of a landscape he might recognize. At night in his narrow cot at the orphanage he would stare into the darkness trying to see this family he had been told about. But, early on, no likenesses came. Sometimes the flames surfaced, and the swirling confusion, then the cold blast of night air. After a few weeks, when the shock began to wear off, he might recall a smile or remember a toy or feel a touch, and it was much worse.

In 1929, Trinity church had added an orphanage—a small, barren annex—and had sponsored the care of dozens of children over the years. By 1948, however, when Patrick and Gillian arrived, state-run institutions were handling most of the need, and the church's orphanage took in just a few children. Only seven lived there that February, under the patient care of Mary Singleton. The fire made Larry number eight.

Larry often felt Mary's eyes on him. She tried to engage him in games with the other children but he refused to let go of his solitude. He recognized it as something he could count on.

One day he was hunched down in the yard, his back against the brick wall of the church building. Through an open window above his head he heard Mary talking to the pastor.

"Reverend, I'm worried about one of our boys, Larry Broadfellow, the one from the fire."

"Causing problems, is he?" Reverend Brannigan had asked Mary.

"Oh, dear, no. Not at all. I wish he would falter once in a while. Poor soul can't seem to get easy. He's alone all the time."

The rough wall cut into Larry's skinny shoulder blades as he pressed in closer, concentrating on every word. He heard dishes clanking, maybe teacups.

"Patrick, you look exhausted."

"Never enough hours in the day, Mary. If the congregation is thinning you have to work extra hard to bring in new people. Then, once you get it thriving again, there are more people to serve than you can handle. Gillian's beat, too, though of course she won't say a word.

"But that's not going to help you. Can you bring the boy over to my office at seven this evening? I'll talk with him. Perhaps we'll need to get some professional help."

"Thank you, Reverend. Victoria can bring him over when she's finished in the kitchen."

LARRY COULD BARELY SWALLOW his dinner that evening, wondering what was going to happen to him later. By the time Victoria, Mary Singleton's helper, came for him, he was nearly paralyzed with anxiety.

"Here 'e is, Rev'rend," Victoria said, depositing him in a stiff-backed chair from which his feet dangled.

The pastor looked up from his reading, then closed the book, carefully drawing the tasseled marker across the page to keep his place.

"How have you been, Victoria?"

She rubbed gently over her swollen belly. "Tired lately, but okay. The doctor says the baby's real healthy. That's the main thing, isn't it? Danny's working two jobs for a bit. We can't wait."

"Thanks for bringing young Larry. Can you come back in a half hour?"

Larry ducked away as she brushed at his hair. "Be good now," she admonished.

The door closed quietly and Larry stared, seeing Patrick Brannigan close up for the first time. He was in the habit of studying grown men, looking for a father. He already loved Mrs. Brannigan. She explained how busy she was with meetings to go to, or social events to arrange, but almost every day she sought Larry out, taking time for a few words.

Reverend Brannigan seemed younger without his robes on. He had a soft face with bushy eyebrows. When he smiled across at Larry, Larry shyly looked down at his own shoes.

The pastor held the Bible out to him. "Would you like to see this? It has some beautiful pictures."

Larry nodded and the minister settled the huge book on his lap. Larry felt the pebbly, embossed leather, his fingers tracing the indented letters. Here, at last, was something familiar. He smiled.

"Do you know the Bible?" the pastor asked. "I mean, aside from your Sunday School lessons."

"I can read it," Larry said proudly. He opened the thick volume and searched through to the book of Matthew. The slick pages wanted to regroup on their own, but he held them firmly and found Matthew

18:22 and 18:23. He glanced up at Reverend Brannigan who was nodding at him to go ahead.

Larry read slowly and deliberately, following the words with an index finger. "Then came Peter to him, and said, Lord, how oft shall my brother sin against me, and I forgive him? Till seven times? Jesus saith unto him, I say not unto thee, until seven times; but until seventy times seven."

A grin split his face after this accomplishment. "My daddy used to make me read that part when my little brother made me mad." A sudden wash of sadness erased his smile and brought tears. Reverend Brannigan jumped up, took the book, and knelt beside Larry's chair, patting his arm. Larry sobbed for several minutes, then the pastor gave him a tissue.

"Most five year-olds can't read," he said. "Does Mary Singleton know that you can?"

Larry shook his head.

"Who taught you?"

Larry shrugged, still struggling for his voice.

"Come with me. We're going to the library."

IN ALL THIS RETROSPECTION, Larry's eyes did not leave Gillian's form. He discovered that each breath moved the bedcovers very slightly and he was grateful for this evidence that she was still with him.

Larry recalled Patrick taking him by the hand and leading him directly from his office to the orphanage's small library. With books in hand, that first spring and summer passed in a moment. By the fall he could read almost anything, and the adventures on the pages compounded until he could escape loneliness at will.

The Filigree Cross

He spent an hour or so every month sitting in Patrick's study talking about stories he did not quite understand. For four years his life consisted of school, reading, and Patrick's patient tutoring.

When Larry turned nine, Patrick approached him about moving to a larger orphanage.

"There's a government home in Madison where they have a dairy, a small farm, a bakery, a laundry. There are a hundred different things you could do," the reverend said. "Not like here. Our place is too small for you, Larry. You're gifted. You need lots of opportunities to find out what you like best."

A sickness crawled in the pit of his stomach. No one really wanted him. The Brannigans had been kind, but he still didn't have a home. At nine years old, he had felt ashamed of the tears that rolled down his cheeks.

Patrick put an arm around his shoulder. "I promise you I will write you once a month. And if, after a good trial, maybe six months, things are not working out, I'll bring you back here."

Suddenly Larry lost all control. He wrapped his arms around Brannigan. He tucked his face into the man's chest, and let out a sob that shook them both. Patrick kissed the top of his head and smoothed his hair. They stood together for several minutes, Brannigan murmuring comforting words.

When Larry regained his composure, he dried his eyes and pulled away. "I'll try, if you really want me to."

"Good boy," Brannigan said. "Come with me."

They moved into the nave of the church and walked part way down the aisle. Brannigan pointed upward. High above them, a model of an old sailing ship hung from the beams. Five feet long with yellowed linen sails, its hull was painted glossy black. Its masts glistened with varnish, the bow pointing toward the altar.

"What did you learn in Sunday School about the ship?" the reverend asked.

"It reminds us to always keep our course to God."

"Good. There are many references in the Bible to Jesus and the disciples crossing stormy seas. In Matthew fourteen, verse twenty-three it speaks about a rising wind and heavy seas."

"That's when Jesus walked on the water," Larry added eagerly. "He calmed the sea and made everything right. Sometimes Jesus comes to me like that. When I'm scared or lonely He makes me feel better."

"And He will be with you wherever you are. You know that, don't you?"

"Yes."

"Then I can send you away and know you'll be okay."

Patrick reached into the wooden pocket on the back of a pew and handed Larry a postcard; on the front was a picture of the ship.

"Keep this with you, son. It will help you remember the Sunday School lesson." Brannigan hugged him again. "And remember that we will always love you, Mrs. Brannigan and Mary and Victoria and me."

A FEW DAYS LATER Mary Singleton planted a kiss on his cheek, dried her eyes, and put him on a bus.

He carried a well-used suitcase. Pinned inside his pants pocket was a letter that identified him and his destination.

Too quickly the streets became foreign. As the bus sped through unfamiliar countryside, fear built in his belly, and Larry slipped the postcard from his jacket pocket. To distract himself from his anxiety, he turned the picture over and read the back.

> *Viking families, whose menfolk were sailors, made replicas of the ships and gave them to the church as votive offerings to ensure the safety of their sons and husbands. The practice of placing a miniature ship in churches has been adopted by some Christian congregations. The ship signifies the congregation's journey toward their heavenly home.*

Clutching the card, he watched the passing landscape take him further away from Reverend Brannigan. He would make sure he did not stay at the new orphanage for long; no matter how much they tried to make him like it, he would not. He would be back in Chicago in six months.

LARRY'S ARM SLIPPED FROM THE ARM of the chair, jerking him awake. He rose stiffly, rubbing his back. Gillian still seemed to be resting easily. He touched the water to her mouth once again, tucked the sheet around her shoulders, and kissed her cheek. "It's Larry. I'll be back soon," he said.

He found Mrs. Daley in the living room. "She's asleep, and I badly need to do the same," he said.

"I'll go to her right away."

Larry walked back upstairs and down the long corridor to the first guest room. He opened the door and saw that Patrick slept soundly. He checked on Sue as well, then found a bed for himself. His own home was just a few hundred yards beyond the mansion, on the same property, but tonight it was too far away. He stripped off his clothes, peeled back crisp bedding, and stretched out. It eased his body but not his mind, and sleep was a long time coming.

CHAPTER FOUR

JOHNNY CAMERON HADN'T BEEN able to coax his grandmother out of bed for four days. She had cried all day and whimpered all night ever since that preacher woman died. Johnny was grateful the home care nurse was due tomorrow; she'd get Gram up, and no nonsense about it.

He carried her breakfast of cereal, coffee, and toast. "After you eat you have to get up, Gram. You'll get all stiff."

She blew her nose. "It doesn't matter. If the world can get along after the death of Gillian Brannigan, it can surely get along without the likes of me."

Johnny set the tray aside and helped her sit up, plumping the pillows. "Don't talk like that. You're younger than she was, and you don't have cancer. And what would I do without you?"

She grabbed at his arm with an urgency that gave her strength. "I want to send some money, as a memorial. Johnny, you have to send it for me."

"Gram, we don't have any to spare. She's gone now. She doesn't need your money."

"Just fifty dollars. Please, Johnny."

Her eyes pleaded with him. He sighed. It was futile to argue. "Twenty, Gram. I'll send twenty. No more than that."

She smiled for the first time in days. "And please find a really nice card. I want to write a note in it."

LARRY ENTERED PATRICK'S STUDY to find Sue already curled into the bend of the largest sofa, her fists bunched under her armpits. She trained her eyes on his face as if he could explain away her grief. When he had nothing to offer, she shifted her gaze to the portrait of Gillian which had been painted when she was in her late sixties.

"Grandma hated posing for that," she said. "She couldn't be still. Now she's still."

"Sue, dear," Patrick offered, "don't think of her that way."

Larry hadn't seen Patrick, a shadow in a corner of the huge room.

"Gillie is as busy as ever, with even more important work to do." He shuffled toward them into the lamplight and dropped into his chair. His eyes blazed, sleepless and tear-free. At the graveside Larry had noticed no physical evidence of Patrick's struggle. Even as her body was lowered, he had stood stock still, his face impassive.

The three of them sat looking at one another. Larry wondered why he had been summoned. Suddenly Patrick pushed himself up from his chair, using his cane for leverage. He traversed the magnificent custom-made carpet with gold crosses woven on a midnight blue background. With one hand he held back the edge of a tapestry, revealing a wall safe. His

The Filigree Cross

fingers moved slowly, his lips murmuring the numbers, then he successfully tumbled the lock and the door swung open.

"Gillie left a letter for each of you."

The envelope he handed to Larry was marked in fat, dark letters: 'Extremely Private.' Larry tucked it into the inside pocket of his coat jacket. Sue dropped her envelope in her lap as if she couldn't bear to touch it. Larry rose and took her hand.

"I'll be all right," she said. "You go. I'll stay with Grandpa."

Looking into Patrick's rheumy eyes, Larry realized he had no sense of the depth of the man's sorrow. "Patrick, you need to rest. Please take those pills the doctor left. Sleep will help."

Patrick's face pulled up on the left side as he spoke. "Stop worrying about me, son. As soon as I'm through arguing with the Lord, I'll rest."

LARRY WALKED THROUGH THE garden, between groomed hedges and lush flower beds, to his own living quarters—a full-sized guest house as well appointed as the mansion.

Though the sun lingered outside, the den, his favorite room, was dark. He hadn't opened the drapes in days. Leather and wood surfaces glowed as the low fire in the grate sent licks of light their way. The walls, dark green in daylight, appeared almost black. On the mantel, on bookshelves and tables, sat years of Larry's handiwork. There were carved ducks, pheasants, owls—all manner of feathered creatures. Not an outdoorsman, Larry had studied paintings and sketches by nature artists. His lifelong hobby had produced professional results. On some of the birds the feathers were etched so finely that it seemed the bird had stopped for only a brief respite and would lift back into flight at any moment. Some wore paint, such as the mallard drake with its silver-tipped feathers layered with teal. Others were varnished so the life-giving wood grains could show through.

The largest carving, and Larry's favorite, was a Copper Pheasant which sat on the floor. Its face was red, with black eyes. A broad, white-speckled back bled into a long and graceful copper tail.

Larry sat down with the pheasant at his feet. He slit the envelope of Gillian's letter with apprehension; this must be the letter for which she had apologized.

Before he could extract the pages, a shiny object fell into his lap. It took him a moment to recognize it as a piece of gold jewelry, for it was mangled as if someone had tried to destroy it. The twisted cross lay in Larry's palm, less substantial than a communion wafer. His own hand was adorned with a thick gold ring, the heft of which still impressed itself after many years of wear. This weightless cross—woven of hair-fine threads—must have been purchased during the dry, dusty years, when jewelry was as scarce as were warm showers.

Larry glanced up, blinking. Did he remember Gillian wearing this? Perhaps. He could see her fingering a pendant of some kind during Patrick's sermons. It must have been very early on, within that first year he joined them on the road, because he recalled that she wore no jewelry most of her life.

Confused, Larry pulled out the letter. Gillian's handwriting was erratic—some was in her usual

The Filigree Cross

flowing style, other parts awkwardly constrained. He wondered if there had been spasms of pain which caused her to struggle for control of her pen. The first words were an admonition to open the letter only in private, and to destroy it immediately after reading it. The command was curt, brooking no argument. Then she began:

> *Dearest Larry,*
> *I love you with all my heart, and I need you to forgive me. Ever since Patrick and I left Trinity church, scurrying away, heads bent in shame, I've lived a terrible lie. After the church spurned him—during all those years we lived hand-to-mouth—I stood by Patrick's side in tents so hot they surely forewarned of hell, and sang glories to a god I'd come to hate.*

Larry re-read the last few lines. Surely, her illness had made her delusional.

> *God allowed Patrick's career to be destroyed by that scandal. You know he is the finest, purest human there is, and god let his church ministry be shattered by the ravings of a foolish woman. You can't imagine his confusion; he thought he must deserve that punishment. I don't know if he has ever fully regained his confidence. All he ever asked from god was insight. Well, that was never enough for me. And then—our sweet Fiona.*

Here, the handwriting became a wild scrawl. Long dashes, underlinings and exclamation points revealed her fury.

> *What kind of a god lets a wonderful young woman go through that?—What kind?—A hateful, spiteful one! He never lets us rest! He never has enough of <u>testing</u>; he's <u>unquenchable</u>.*

Larry flinched at the harshness of the words, but the next paragraph appeared to have been written on a better day.

> *I addressed the faithful while wearing this cross, a gift from Patrick. I didn't realize at the time how well it suited me. It is a transparent symbol, without substance. The day I crushed it, it folded like my faith, offering no resistance. Of course, I carried on for Patrick, because he'd never have been able to understand. But I am a fraud, Larry. For a long while I've been watching you carefully, and I wonder if you're not doing what I did. Are we matching charlatans?*

Larry's fists clenched, crumpling the letter. It was impossible. He pictured her as he'd seen her over the years during countless broadcasts. She had stood, the Bible spread open in her hands, her face glowing as she praised the Lord in song. Her lovely voice had always brought him hope that one day he would find a way to believe again.

The Filigree Cross

On her deathbed Gillian had whispered, "I'm sorry about the letter." Had she meant to take the words back? Or was she simply sorry that what she wrote was true? He spread the pages flat and scanned them again, unwilling to accept the words, angry with her.

Hadn't she understood? He wasn't a fake, he was merely a conduit. Some people's faith, however strong, seemed to need routing. Why else did they come to him? What did it matter if he had no faith of his own? They had it. If they thought he somehow facilitated a connection with God, and were satisfied, wasn't that enough?

The letter had another page but he couldn't read any more. He stuffed it and the cross back into the envelope and slid them under a stack of magazines by his chair.

What if Gillian were right? What if he had been taking the prayers of those millions of faithful and thrusting their aspirations into oblivion? He saw himself on stage strutting and shouting, promising redemption. The image of himself prancing changed to one of a mindless puppet throwing out-of-control limbs at all angles, the painted smile denying its own stupidity.

AFTER A SLEEPLESS NIGHT, he was not in any better condition to face the rest of Gillian's letter. But as he read, he found the worst was over. She had asked two specific favors of him. He memorized her requests and stood by the fireplace trying to burn the letter as she had asked. As awful as it was, he imagined her fingers touching the paper, and he couldn't make himself put the envelope to the flames. He would keep the letter until all her wishes had been fulfilled, and since that could take a lifetime, maybe he'd never have to part with it. He walked to his office and locked her confession in a metal box in his desk.

GILLIAN'S FIRST REQUEST had to do with the ministry. She had anticipated an outpouring of gifts to the church in her name and asked that Larry not allow McLaren and Technicolor to use her death as a fundraiser. 'I was false in life,' she wrote. 'Don't let me be false in death.'

Larry reached for the phone and dialed Tech's home. There was no answer. If not at home, Tech would almost surely be at the office, even on a weekend.

Tech answered the call cheerfully, his voice dropping when he recognized Larry's voice.

"It was a wonderful service, Larry. Gillian would be pleased. How are you doing? How's the family holding up?"

"Patrick won't rest. I expect he'll just collapse soon. As for Sue, I don't know. She's struggling. We all are."

"Yes, it's a real blow to the church," Tech said. Then added, "To all of us."

"What are you doing at the office today?"

"We're swamped. Letters and calls are flooding in. It's bedlam down here."

"Well, I can make your life easier. I assume money is coming in, too."

"Tons of it. Everyone wants to feel a part of her memorial."

The Filigree Cross

"Well, you just print up a form letter that says Gillian asked for no donations in connection with her death and stuff it into a return envelope with the check. If all the office staff pitches in, it can't take too long."

"What?" Tech all but shouted. "That's crazy. Gillian was always humble, but never so humble as to refuse money. She knew the ministry has no legs without money."

"Tech, it was one of her last wishes. She left me a letter asking that favor. I have to honor her request."

There was a long pause. Larry heard a mumbled conversation taking place behind a covered mouthpiece.

Tech came back on the line. "I've just talked to Mark. He agrees with me. We think that's crazy. We're talking a lot of money. We can use it well, satisfy some of the charter obligations. The Bosnian Children's Fund, for instance. We can do some real good here, Larry."

"Tech, we're sending it back. I assume any checks already received have been targeted to a separate account."

"Of course."

"Then that will make them easy to find and return."

TECH REPLACED THE RECEIVER and turned to Mark, shaking his head. "He's adamant."

"Well, what about Patrick? What does Patrick think? Who made Larry king of the damn hill?"

"You know Patrick doesn't give a fig about money. Anyway, apparently it's something Gillian requested." He sighed. "What a pain."

Mark's voice fell to just above a whisper. "Look, everyone's under a lot of stress right now. Maybe Larry will change his mind. What about we sit on it for a while?"

"What do you mean?"

Mark checked to see the office door was closed and put both hands on the edge of Tech's desk. "Who works harder and longer around here, you or Larry?"

"No contest. Me."

"Me, too. And who among us three has a salary in six digits?"

Tech studied Mark's face to be sure he was understanding what his friend was saying. "You mean, we move the money for now. So that, once everyone's grief has passed and people are thinking more clearly—"

"Exactly. Perfect. Technicolor, you're an effin' genius."

"Now, now. No cursing."

"What's the safest way to do this?" Mark asked.

Tech gave it some thought. "We'll return everything over fifty dollars. The smaller donations are far less likely to be followed up on."

Tech and Mark made a point of asking key people in the office for input into the text of the letter that would accompany the checks they had to return. Then they suggested that it would streamline things if all money sent on Gillian's behalf was routed to Tech's secretary, Theresa. His office would handle the refunds.

MAUREEN CAMERON'S CARD landed on Tech's desk amid hundreds. He hastily ripped it

The Filigree Cross

open—the one with two white doves on a gold-leaf background. Gillian's death had been a windfall for Hallmark. He removed the twenty dollars and checked the computer; she was in there. He punched a few keys and generated a receipt for tax purposes that would go to her immediately, along with the church's standard thank-you letter. As he added the check to the deposit slip for the new account, he scanned the spidery writing that started below the printed message on the card and carried over to the back. This woman wanted prayers said for her grandson, Johnny, who had been born to a drug-addicted mother. She explained how Johnny spent all his spare time caring for her. Tech grimaced; he didn't like to be reminded that faith was all some people had.

A second note was squeezed below hers, in a tighter hand: *You'd better send my Gram a real nice thank you. She's in bed crying over Mrs. Brannigan.*

Tech glanced at the massive stack of envelopes on his desk, hesitated only a moment, then tossed the card into the overflowing waste basket.

JOHNNY MADE GRAM'S FAVORITE lunch, tuna and macaroni salad. He had spruced up the kitchen, even washed the windows and wiped off the toaster to please her.

"Gram, you've gotten too skinny grieving over that lady. Eat up."

Maureen Cameron pushed her plate away and pulled an envelope from the pocket of her skirt.

"This is what I got from them." She handed it to Johnny. It was the ministry's standard thank-you form letter with an IRS receipt. "It's just like all the others."

"But there's nothing here about your request for prayers," he said. "Nothing about a memorial for that woman."

Maureen corrected him sharply. "Don't say 'that woman.' Her name is Gillian Brannigan. And I guess the twenty dollars wasn't enough. We should have sent fifty, like I told you in the first place."

Johnny reached out to touch her hand. "Gram, the amount of money shouldn't matter."

She stiffened and withdrew her hand. "Look at the time. You're going to be late for work."

He gulped the last of his salad and grabbed a jacket, not knowing if he was more angry with her or with the church.

Three weeks later, when Johnny read the bank statement, he panicked. A canceled check for two thousand dollars lay before him. His grandmother had sent the Church of God's Love more than half of their entire savings.

While his grandmother snored through her afternoon nap, Johnny searched the desk in her bedroom and found an address for Larry Broadfellow.

THERESA CLARK, TECHNICOLOR'S secretary and lover, opened the envelope addressed to the Reverend Larry Broadfellow, thinking of all the people who were fooled. Though Larry was always careful not to claim any credentials, people assumed he was an ordained minister, as she had herself.

When she joined the organization three years earlier, Theresa's goal had been the seduction of the good reverend. His television persona had mesmerized her, filling her nights with distinctly unchristian

The Filigree Cross

thoughts. The idea of bringing a man who was so close to God completely down to earth added the drama she liked. As it turned out, Larry was not drawn to thin, dramatic brunettes. He was usually polite to her, but the closer she tried to get, the more she felt him pushing her away. No one in the office seemed to know anything about his private life. Occasionally, when he ignored her and made her angry, she even wondered whether he might be gay. However, his walking into a room unexpectedly could still make her breath catch, and she had not given up hope.

Theresa read the letter in her hand then went immediately into Tech's office.

"This looks like trouble," she said. "Came addressed to Larry, marked Personal."

Tech swiveled away from a computer screen filled with columns of numbers. His eyes ranged over her taut body. "I love that sweater," he said.

She merely squinted her eyes a bit. Compliments, if that was one, rolled off his tongue like marbles off a mirror. "Well you won't like this." She leaned across the steel desk and handed him the letter.

Tech read it over, frowned slightly, then shrugged.

He tossed the letter toward her. "So send the kid the two thousand dollars back. Grandma got carried away. It happens."

"Tech, forget the numbers for once. Read between the lines. The money's only part of it. Grandma wanted proper recognition of her earlier twenty dollar donation. That one was for Gillian; obviously it must have gone into the new account."

Tech began to see uncomfortable possibilities. Aside from him, only Mark and Theresa knew about the slush account. The balance had reached over three hundred thousand dollars when they shut it down. If they didn't handle this exactly right, if they offended this kid further, he would find a way to get directly to Larry, or God forbid, Brannigan.

Tech looked at the return address.

"Don't we go to Minneapolis soon?" He turned to the computer, bringing a calendar up on the monitor. "Early in October." He looked up at Theresa. "First we send the two thousand back and apologize about her receiving the form letter—computer glitch, whatever. Then we invite them to the Minneapolis service. Front row seats, limo pickup, all the trimmings."

Theresa hesitated. "I don't know. They seem like decent, simple folks. It might be too much. The grandson sounds skeptical enough already."

"Okay, you're right, as usual. The limo's over the top. I don't have a sense for these things."

Theresa knew he was always embarrassed when she was right.

He began waving his arms like a traffic cop, making fun of her. "Cancel the limo. Let them make their own way through the streets, hunt a half hour for a parking spot, fight their way through the crowded masses down to the front row. See if I care. They'll appreciate us all the more."

Theresa laughed at his performance. Before she turned to leave, she paused, letting her eyes range over his chest. "I love that fuchsia shirt, especially with the gold suspenders."

THE SECOND REQUEST IN GILLIAN'S letter haunted Larry. Of course there was nothing he could

The Filigree Cross

refuse her, but this would tear him apart. She'd asked him to take her place, regularly visiting Fiona at the clinic.

He had been going to see Fiona only once or twice a year; that was all the exposure his heart could bear. Each time he was freshly ripped open, and slow to heal. He saw her young again, and her laugh took him back more than twenty years in a split second. Her nearness kept him from completely loving any other woman, yet she was completely lost to him. Every visit expanded his loneliness.

Gillian's letter reminded him, unnecessarily, that Fiona's forty-fifth birthday was coming up. He and Sue were to take her a gift wrapped in pink paper—a book of Renoir or Degas paintings perhaps—and homemade cookies. Well, Gillian had conceded, he could buy some, but not too fancy. Fiona might notice they were store-bought.

Larry slumped forward on his desk, his forehead resting on folded arms. He had told himself a thousand times that fate was only a word that gave substance to circumstance and whim. All lives turned on a glance, or a blink. He had told himself a hundred times it wasn't his fault. But was there a moment when he had blinked, when he lost the chance to save Fiona?

Larry let the years fall away. He knew he was in for a torturous ride, but he hadn't taken it for a while. And he knew the thrill was almost worth the pain.

Marlene Baird

PART TWO

1970 – 1972

A Wastrel's Journey

Marlene Baird

The Filigree Cross

CHAPTER FIVE

THE DAY HE'D FIRST SEEN HER he was walking on the shoulder of the highway, dust puffing up around his already filthy tennis shoes. His stomach churned with hunger and cheap wine, and when he belched the raw sourness threatened to choke him. His flimsy shirt stunk of dried puke. On his left ran the two-lane highway, heat shimmering it to waves in the distance. To his right, fields of grain, yellow, sharply dry.

He pulled his straw cowboy hat off, allowing the ring of sweat to cool his forehead. He shoved his fist inside the hat, trying to pop the crushed crown back into shape, but it was permanently bent, no doubt from his falling asleep on the bus. Then he remembered he'd left his shopping bag behind.

"Damn!" He slapped a skinny thigh. Probably that grinning old woman across the aisle had it now, along with all his books and the family of ducks he'd been carving. She'd probably throw away Steinbeck and keep the ducks, if she couldn't sell them. He patted his back pocket, feeling for the whittling knife. It was there. That eased his pain a little. The loss was his own fault. He had boarded the bus in a drunken stupor, an easy way to forget things. Forgetting was often his goal.

He had disembarked when the driver shook his shoulder. "Hey, fella. You've run out of fare."

The man had no clue just how right he was.

The town where the bus dumped him was far too quiet, its streets sparsely peopled with intent, sober citizens. Feeling like a freak, he headed out on the highway. When he'd walked about a mile, he began to feel a bit better. The air smelled earthy and clean; he felt pleased that he could still appreciate such things. A road sign read, "Thanks for visiting Morriston." He tipped his hat. "You're very welcome."

He searched the horizon in both directions for traffic, but pickings looked slim. He had no destination, only hope of a ride from someone who would offer him a couple of dollars when they dropped him off. He had his tale of woe pretty much perfected, and it touched many people. He was an orphan and a vet—a good line, and even true. He smiled to himself. He had enough wine still in his system for smiling.

It was so quiet that the rhythm of his steps set up a cadence in his brain. Left, right, left, right. He started to march. He was back in basic training, swinging his arms, stepping lively. Only now, with each swing of an arm, he raised his middle finger in salute to the drill sergeant he'd hated so thoroughly. He pictured the man's face screwed up in disbelief as Larry gave him the finger over and over, left, right, left, right, and he

The Filigree Cross

started to laugh. "Take that, Mahoney!" he said, punching the air with his raised finger.

The screeching of brakes and the blare of a car's horn jerked him out of his silly march. He lunged back to the shoulder of the road, trying to get his balance as air rushed around him and a car fender brushed against his jeans. A car veered onto the shoulder in front of him and stopped. Once the dust settled he could see that the car was an ancient Oldsmobile, dinged and scratched, rendered even more forlorn-looking by an unprofessional paint job.

A young girl emerged and ran back toward him.

"Are you okay?" she exclaimed, worry all over her pretty face. "You lunged right out in front of me."

Larry tried to stand straight.

"Sorry. I was lost in thought. I'm fine." She had wonderful legs thrusting out of shorts and her light auburn hair was pulled into a long pony tail. "Are you old enough to drive?"

She smiled. "In most states. I'm sixteen and a few months. Do you need a ride somewhere?"

"Why would a pretty little lady like you go around picking up strangers?"

"My folks hate it, but I do it all the time. I don't give everyone a ride; I can tell about people."

"And in two seconds you've decided that I'm harmless?" He couldn't take his eyes from hers. They radiated everything wonderful about youth—enthusiasm, trust, invincibility. Wonderful feelings he'd never known in all his life, except through his reading.

"No," she said. "I haven't decided about you at all." She pointed to the crest of a small hill that rose beyond the car. "My folks are just over there. I thought if you needed help, I could arrange something."

Larry shaded his eyes with his hand and saw the top of a tent sticking up.

"You in a traveling circus?"

She giggled. It was the happiest sound he'd heard in years. "Some people call it that. But my dad would kill me if he heard me say so."

His head was starting to ache, and he needed to belch again. "So what is it, really, that tent?"

"It's a gospel meeting place."

His eyebrows must have risen visibly, because she laughed at him. "Oh, my dad's not a faith healer or anything like that. And we're not holy rollers if that's what you're thinking. He's a really good preacher and people come to hear him." She glanced at her watch. "In a half hour they'll start arriving. We'll have about two hundred tonight, probably. Why don't you come?"

The suggestion was so ludicrous, Larry almost laughed aloud. He wanted to ask why, if her dad was such a good preacher, he didn't have a nice church instead of a tent, but that would be too rude, even for him. And her face was so sincere.

"I'll bet you've got nothing else to do. Come on. We serve sandwiches and coffee."

"What kind of sandwiches?"

"Ham or peanut butter. The hams go pretty fast. You'll have to be quick."

"I'm faster than I look, young lady."

"I'll meet you in front of the tent in five minutes." She jumped back in the car. The engine hesitated before it caught, then she pulled out very carefully and drove off with a backward wave.

The Filigree Cross

Once over the hill, Larry saw a four-sided tent maybe thirty feet by thirty. Fat green and white stripes ran up the walls, tapering to the pointed roof. A wooden sign planted in the weeds announced that the Church of God's Love welcomed everyone, and it promised salvation to boot. Larry grunted. Promises had long been removed from his list of things to count on. Along with religion. Especially religion.

The girl waved and ran toward him as soon as Larry started up the rutted gravel road. She'd changed into a long skirt and a blouse that hid her pretty breasts. She took his hand. Hers was soft, and as delicate as a bird's wing.

"Come on, I'll get you a couple of sandwiches before everyone arrives," she said.

The tent held rows of folding chairs facing a shallow, wooden stage which boasted one microphone and a guitar leaning against a stool. Flap doors on either side of the tent were pinned open, but this did not produce a badly needed breeze. A string of lights draped from the overhead braces. Larry heard the hum of a generator.

A middle-aged woman, strands of lovely red hair falling loose around her face, entered through one of the side doors, struggling with a huge tray of sandwiches. She headed for a table that ran against one side of the tent. The girl let go of Larry's hand and rushed to help.

"Mom, I've brought someone to the meeting. This is . . . oh, I don't know your name."

Larry swept off his hat and bowed to the older woman. "Larry Broadfellow, ma'am."

Marlene Baird

The woman's mouth fell open. "Larry Broadfellow? From Chicago?"

Larry hesitated, unsure that admitting to any information about his background was a good idea. "At one time."

The tray slipped from her hands. The girl tried to rescue the sandwiches but they slid to the ground in a heap. The woman seemed to collapse, then groped her way to a chair and sat down.

Her eyes grew round and wide as she studied his face. Her hand went to her chest, then she burst into a smile. "Patrick will die! Patrick will absolutely die!" She jumped back up and hugged Larry. Then she held him at arm's length. "Larry, it's Gillian. You don't recognize me. Gillian Brannigan."

Larry searched her face. Yes, it could be her, much as he wished otherwise. After Reverend Brannigan had essentially abandoned him at the second orphanage where he had been so miserable, Larry had tried to scrub every memory of the Brannigans from his mind. He had received only one short note from them saying that they were leaving Chicago. After that, Larry's anxious letters were returned, unopened.

Larry glanced at the girl. Their daughter, now sixteen, must have been born after they sent Larry away, and they had simply forgotten him.

Larry looked around the tent, glad to find that the pastor was not inside. He had time to escape. He spun on his heels and headed for the exit. He broke into a run as he cleared the doorway. He heard Gillian Brannigan calling him to come back and urging the girl to find her father.

The Filigree Cross

Instead, the girl chased him and easily outran him. She grabbed the back of his shirt.

"What's the matter? Come back."

He jerked angrily away from her hold. "Leave me alone."

"No." She held on to him again. "What's going on?"

He twisted around to yell at her, to tell her that he hated her parents, had hated them for years, but her face registered such concern and innocence he could not. Over her shoulder he saw Patrick running toward them. He was no longer the young pastor of Larry's memory, but a slow-moving middle-aged man with deep lines in his face.

"Larry!" Patrick called, extending his arms, breathing hard. He folded Larry in a hug. "Don't run," he begged between gasps. "Don't run away."

Larry wanted to push him off, but the embrace engendered that thread of love he'd had for Patrick as a boy—the only true love he could remember knowing. Larry slumped against the older man. He hated himself for his weakness and hid his face in his hands as hot tears came.

"Come, boy. People are arriving. Come into the trailer."

As the girl and Patrick all but dragged him behind the tent, Larry realized how dirty and unkempt he must look against these two. The sleeve of Patrick's white shirt entwined with his own soiled one. Patrick smelled of aftershave and toothpaste. Larry clamped his mouth shut against the release of alcoholic breath.

They climbed two bent aluminum steps into a small travel trailer which, Larry saw, was hitched to a pickup truck. Gillian Brannigan was suddenly there, handing him a cup of coffee, and apologizing that they didn't have time to talk just now.

"Fiona, please go out and greet people," she asked her daughter. The girl glanced at Larry, her face registering confusion, then left. Gillian explained that she had to prepare some more food and that Patrick had to check on the public address system.

"Promise me you won't leave," Gillian asked. "Not before we've had a chance to explain."

Patrick added, "Don't go, son. Hear us out."

Alone, Larry laid back against the trailer's lumpy sofa, his head bumping the wall. Soon the noise of cars arriving was replaced by the strumming of the guitar from inside the tent, then a sweet voice beginning a hymn.

Hesitantly, the audience began to join in, and soon their voices rose in unison. Curious, he left the trailer, entered the tent, and took a chair set off at one side. Body heat had raised the temperature inside another fifteen degrees. He pulled at his shirt collar and rolled his sleeves.

After the hymn Fiona jumped down from the stage, and Patrick took the microphone. He spoke quietly, just as Larry remembered, meeting the eyes of everyone close enough to him. He read a short passage of scripture then spoke more personally. "The Lord has brought us together. Isn't it wonderful?" Patrick paused, waiting for an answer. Heads nodded. A few mumbled their agreement, some murmuring quiet Amens.

Patrick leaned forward, addressing the people in the front row. "I feel Him here with us." He reached

The Filigree Cross

toward them. "Do you feel it? There's a strength to the air, a strong thread joining us together." He straightened and closed his eyes for a moment. "Here, Lord," he uttered in a husky voice. He tilted his head back and patted his heart. "Here, Lord, is where we need you."

The audience sat still until, as Patrick remained silent, they began to put their hands over their hearts and close their eyes. Smiles spread across their faces.

Patrick's chest rose and fell as he breathed deeply. His voice was guttural, a hoarse whisper. "Come fill us, Lord. We are dry, empty vessels. We are thirsty. Fill us."

Larry felt tears again. *What the hell's wrong with me today? I need a drink, that's what. Damn cry baby.*

Patrick opened his arms wide and looked into the eyes of the crowd. A peacefulness shone from his face.

"I can feel Him. And I know you can, too."

Larry scanned the audience as discreetly as possible. An inordinate number of people wore Patrick's same serene expression as they folded their hands in their laps.

The service lasted just over an hour, and Patrick didn't lose his audience once. At about midpoint Fiona and Gillian walked the aisle, accepting donations that were dropped into small fishbowls, each lined with a piece of blue felt.

After the service many people embraced Patrick and the two women. Then they talked quietly among themselves as they moved outside, some dropping extra donations into a bowl on their way. Larry noticed a small table near the entrance on which donations of food had been placed. A large ham dominated the collection.

LATER, SITTING ON THE TRAILER steps, Gillian wouldn't let go of Larry's hand. He wanted to pull it away, but she kept patting it. Patrick sat on a folding chair, Fiona at her father's feet.

"Now, son, I must explain," Patrick began. "That last day, when I talked you into leaving Chicago—" Patrick sought Larry's eyes, but Larry cast his gaze on the scruffy grass at his feet.

"Do you remember?" Patrick asked.

Larry nodded his head without moving his eyes.

"Well, that day a most unexpected event took place."

Larry looked accusingly at Patrick. Nothing the man said could absolve him from the abandonment of a young boy.

"Do you remember putting your arms around me?" Patrick continued earnestly. "And me hugging you because you were upset at leaving?"

Larry waited.

"A woman who was in the church that day, doing housekeeping chores, saw that embrace and deliberately misinterpreted it."

Larry stared at Patrick. "Misinterpreted it?" As understanding came to him his jaw dropped. "You can't mean she thought we—"

"I don't know what she actually thought, but that is what she reported to everyone who would listen."

Larry shook his head, then, embarrassed, glanced at Fiona. She studied her father and blinked as if trying to absorb the meaning of the words.

The Filigree Cross

Gillian gripped Larry's hand more firmly as she spoke. "She was a young, lonely widow. When Patrick counseled her she fell in love with him, or thought she had. The situation became so touchy that Patrick could no longer visit with her unless there were others present. She perceived this as him turning away from her, and, hating him for that, she embellished what she had seen."

Patrick continued. "You must understand, son, I had to break off contact with you. There were all manner of rumors being spread. I didn't dare contact you. I'd have given them more fuel for their fire. The church might have even brought you back for questioning, God forbid. What would your young mind have made of charges like that?"

Still confused, Larry asked, "Why didn't you stay and fight?"

Gillian pressed his hand and nodded; clearly that was still her own question.

"If I'd fought it, it would have become public. There would have been no end of bad publicity for the church, and I'd already lost credibility with my congregation. Sometimes a mere accusation is enough; most people never get that out of their minds. I couldn't bear not to be trusted." He paused for a moment, remembering. "The people who were important to me believed me. That was enough."

Fiona finally found her voice. "She must have been a very sick woman. Why would anyone believe her?"

"There'd been a truly wicked scandal involving a choir master just the year before," Patrick explained. "The church was under terrible scrutiny. If anything, I was to blame for not being more circumspect."

Gillian jerked her hand from Larry's and slapped the step of the trailer. "She was a witch," she said vehemently.

Patrick gave her a warning look. "Now, Gillie, if the Lord can forgive, you can too."

"I've never pretended to be as strong as God."

"Oh, but you are. I know it." He smiled at her with complete love. "I'm not sure even He could have made two batches of sandwiches out of the little we had available tonight. You've been working miracles for years."

Gillian flushed, pleased at her husband's admiration.

"Larry," Patrick said, "can you ever forgive me? I've thought about you hundreds of times. You were such a bright boy. I was sure you would be all right; told myself that you would go to a wonderful family in time. Were you never adopted out of that second orphanage?"

Larry paused, scenes flashing rapidly across his mind. He began slowly, judging as he went along how much to tell. "On two Sundays a month, couples would visit the home and look us over. If we passed muster they might take us to their home for a week's trial."

Larry heard sarcasm and pain in his voice, even after all those years. Maybe he could talk about the Perkinses who wanted another pair of hands in their dry cleaning shop, where Larry ate leftovers and their two children taunted him unmercifully about having no real family. Luckily they had tired of his crying and sent him back to the orphanage.

He definitely couldn't say anything about the others, whose names he wouldn't even let himself

The Filigree Cross

remember. He had just turned eleven. Who would have believed that the tall, attractive couple who visited the orphanage dressed for church, clean as spring rain and always smiling, were monsters?

After a week in their house, he was sent to sleep, not on his bed, but in a room he had thought must be only for guests. Oddly, it had no windows, but Larry relished the bed's comfort and cleanliness, stretching his long legs between smooth sheets. The pillow was scented like a flower. A small desk in one corner held a beautiful plaster cast of Jesus on the cross, and a candle sputtered in the dark.

He fell asleep almost immediately, but woke suddenly, struggling to breath. The man's six-foot bulk was stretched over Larry's slim body. Larry flailed with his arms and legs, but the man simply outwaited him. After a few minutes Larry's arms ached from pushing at the man's mass; his legs became heavy logs from kicking out; his neck weakened from struggling against the meaty hand clamped over his mouth. As Larry experienced a shame beyond his imagination, the man called loudly and desperately, for God. Larry, too, wondered where He was.

As soon as the man left the room, Larry tried to escape, but the door was locked. In the morning, shaking with fear, he dressed, and ran for the highway. The woman caught up with him in her car. She agreed to return him to the home, but not before she warned him about talking. Warned him good. She needn't have worried; no amount of coercion could have forced him to utter a single word.

Back at the orphanage, he ran to his room. Richard and Brian, his roommates, watched, frightened, as he threw clothes from his drawer, desperately searching for something. All the while he groaned aloud, tears streaming down his face. In a far corner he found the postcard of the sailing ship. He tore it into dozens of pieces, yelling, "You lied! You lied!"

LARRY SLOWLY BROUGHT HIMSELF back to the little group sitting at the doorway to the trailer. They were waiting patiently. He had carried the hate for too many years, too many miles. Patrick had done what he'd thought best for him. He and Gillian didn't have to know how terribly it all turned out.

"No, I never was adopted," he finally answered, "but it really wasn't so bad after I got reconciled to being there. I learned a lot. And I had one really good friend. Richard liked being at the orphanage and had no intention of being adopted out. On visiting Sundays he would make himself as unattractive as possible. I saw him once take off his shoes and socks and pick energetically at his toenails."

Patrick laughed, and Fiona said, "Yuk!"

"Or he would act like a dolt, using poor grammar, or cuss when no one from the orphanage was within earshot. But he was a great pal, and I missed him a lot after he left. A couple who worked a farm came one day, and for some reason Richard took a liking to them, and he went with them. I guess he was about thirteen then. I got letters from him; he seemed really happy."

"Seemed? Haven't you kept in touch?" Gillian asked.

Larry hesitated. This was beginning to sound like a poor-me act. "No. After I got out of the service, I went

The Filigree Cross

to visit and found he'd been killed in a tractor accident."

"Oh, dear, your best friend," Gillian muttered.

Larry attempted to lighten his tone. "Oh, it's not so bad. Since getting out of the navy I've been wandering around, seeing the country." It sounded feeble. He grunted, chiding himself. "Well, actually, I guess I haven't come very far in all these years. When Mary Singleton sent me off on the bus, I believe I had at least a small suitcase. Today I lost my shopping bag."

"Well, the Lord has sent you back to us again, thank heaven," Patrick said. He hesitated, glancing at the ground before continuing. Larry thought he saw some embarrassment in Patrick's face. "We badly need help, Larry," he said. "Your coming along is a blessing. I'd sure appreciate it if you would stay on with us."

Larry felt the grip of responsibility tightening his gut. They were not quite finished rescuing him.

"When we arrive in a new town, we hire a couple of fellows to help put up the tent, and then they come back to take it down. But the packing and unpacking is backbreaking work." He glanced at Gillian and Fiona. "My two ladies work so hard, it makes me feel bad."

Jesus. He should have seen this coming. He should have just kept on shuffling down that dusty road, ham sandwiches or not. Larry Broadfellow—part of a traveling ministry. It was absurd.

"Thanks a lot, but no."

Disappointment immediately clouded Patrick's eyes.

"I wouldn't be good for you. You have no idea what you'd be getting. I've picked up some bad habits along the way."

"Such as?" Gillian asked.

"Drinking, for one."

"People have been known to stop," Gillian said.

"Well, I'm not sure I want to."

He stood, towering over the three of them. He bent to pick up his hat from the step of the trailer. The thought of being trapped in this insular family made him suddenly desperate for a whiskey.

"Look, I really appreciate the offer, but it's not in my plans. It's wonderful to have met up with you again, but I think I'll just head back to town."

Gillian jumped up. "But after all this time, you can't just leave."

"Gillie, he's a grown man," Patrick offered.

Larry winced at the pain in the man's voice. They meant well; they cared about him.

Gillian straightened her shoulders, then spoke evenly. "Then, would you let Fiona drive you back to town? I need her to pick up a few things for our dinner. Maybe you could see her safely back on the road after her shopping."

Without waiting for his answer, she pulled some bills from her pocket and handed them to Fiona. "Get bread, eggs, potatoes, and some fruit."

Gillian pointedly looked at her watch. "It shouldn't take you much more than a half hour."

AS SOON AS THE CAR WAS ON THE highway Larry felt exhilarated by a sense of freedom. Fiona sat up straight, hands correctly on either side of the wheel,

The Filigree Cross

studying the road before her as if some impediment might suddenly pop up out of the asphalt.

"You're a careful driver for being so young," Larry said.

"Thanks. I just got my license. My dad taught me. I feel awful lucky to have my folks after hearing about your life. It must have been terrible."

"Well, I'm sure lots of people have been through worse."

"I wish you'd stay with us. Dad really needs help and we can't afford to pay anyone right now."

No pay. That hadn't been mentioned. Well, that definitely sealed the deal.

"You going through hard times?" he asked.

"Yeah, kinda bad." Then she smiled. "But we're eating regularly. Nothing fancy, but there's usually enough. And we haven't had anything stolen for a while."

"Like what?"

"The generator. We had to replace it two months ago."

Her tone was matter-of-fact. She wasn't putting it on him, but guilt was creeping up anyway.

"Can I ask you some questions about the ministry?" Larry asked.

"Sure, anything," Fiona said easily.

"If you move every week, how do people know where to find you?"

"First, we make almost the same circuit every summer so a lot of people look for us. Also, Dad sometimes writes ahead, to place newspaper ads, though we haven't had the money to do that lately. Mostly, it's by word of mouth."

She unlocked her eyes from the road and glanced his way. "When I saw you on the highway today I was coming back from town where I put fliers in store windows if the owners agreed. I tacked some to telephone poles and handed out lots of them to passers-by on the street."

This was a labor-intensive operation if ever there was one, Larry thought.

"You must go to school."

"Oh, sure. We'll be on the road the rest of the summer. Then we pick a place to settle for the winter. I've gone to school in seven states. Other than the military kids, that must be some kind of record." She grinned proudly. "But the winter's are really hard on Dad. He's only happy when he's traveling and preaching."

They drove in silence for a few moments, Larry pondering the fact that she'd had no chance to make long-time friends. They had one thing in common.

A slow-moving line of railway cars on the edge of town kept them waiting at the crossing. Larry caught her examining him. Finally her curiosity got the better of her manners.

"Are you part Indian?"

"I guess. Lots of people have mentioned that I look like I could be. But I don't know anything about my family history."

"How old are you, anyway?"

"Twenty-six going on eighty."

Fiona shrugged. "Twenty-six isn't that old."

"Depends on what you've been doing for all those years."

The Filigree Cross

The caboose departed and Fiona carefully guided them across the tracks. Even at ten miles an hour, the back end of the Oldsmobile scraped metal as the car jounced on the other side of the shallow grade. The shocks were totally gone.

"You really don't have an apartment or anything in town?" Fiona asked.

"I got off the bus this morning and didn't even know where I was. And I hardly remember where I got on."

"Have you ever had a home of your own?"

"Not for more than a few months. Don't seem to know how to make a place a home. Your family travels all the time. Don't you feel displaced?"

She smiled. "That trailer is our home. It's as solid as any house with a yard and trees. It's cozy with the three of us sleeping in there, though sometimes I use the back seat of the car so my folks can have some privacy."

It took a while to find a grocery store open so late. Once inside, Larry's eyes immediately wandered toward the shelves of liquor. He swallowed a mouthful of saliva.

"Do you want some beer?" Fiona asked.

"Oh, hell, always."

"Is that because you have so little else?" The question was impertinent, but her tone was not. Her eyes, glistening under the harsh store lights, softened with real concern. She touched his arm, stopping them in the aisle. "Maybe if you stayed on with us, you know, had a kind of home."

She stared at him, honest and innocent, totally unaware of her beauty, her sheltered youth. Every

Marlene Baird

sinew in Larry's throat tightened. Her narrow hand lay like hope on his sleeve. He stood in a podunk town in an all-night grocery store, at the crossroads of his life. He felt rooted to the grimy linoleum. It would take a gargantuan effort to break free.

CHAPTER SIX

LARRY BROUGHT AN EXTRA CHAIR from inside the tent. Neither Gillian nor Patrick had seemed surprised at his return, nor did they say anything. The trailer was too cramped for four people to eat inside, so they sat on folding chairs under the stars, with plates of fried potatoes and scrambled eggs on their laps.

The dusty-sweet smell of wheat stalks filled the air.

"Does the farmer rent you this space?" Larry asked.

"Sometimes we have to pay," Gillian said, "but this one's free. We come here twice every summer, and Mr. Rollins leaves this corner unplanted for us."

"How long will you stay?"

"We'll do our last service Sunday afternoon. We usually try to set up mid-week and stay through Sunday. That gives us enough travel time."

Larry realized he wasn't sure what state he was in. He could have easily slept while the bus went through a border change.

"Do you usually stay in this area in the summer?"

Patrick answered. "Iowa is good to us. We like the heart of the country. These are all good folks.

Marlene Baird

Sometimes I feel like I'm preaching to the choir since so many people who come out belong to conventional congregations. They're curious as to whether they're missing something there, and they are." He put his plate on the ground beside him and picked up his coffee cup. "I've preached inside a church and outside, and I can tell you there's more honesty and devotion under a tent."

Gillian stood and stretched, bracing the small of her back with her hands. In the dim light the dark circles under her eyes were very pronounced. Larry had no doubt she worked as hard as any of them, and carried most of the worry.

"I'm for bed," she said. "Let's clean up in the morning. Patrick, will you just stack everything for me?"

She reached for Fiona's hand. "Come on, love."

The women fetched towels from inside the trailer and headed up the gravel road.

"Where are they going?" Larry asked Patrick.

"The Rollinses invite us to bathe at the house. But I usually go to the campground down the road. It has a shower. Only twenty-five cents."

The men cleaned up the cramped kitchen. Larry had to hunch over to keep from bumping his head on the overhead storage cabinets while he dried the dishes. He watched Patrick, fascinated. "How can you wash so many dishes in so little water, and get them clean?"

"Practice. You get real careful with water," he explained. "It's bulky, and we need to watch the weight for the vehicles. The Oldsmobile has to pull the flatbed with the tent and all the gear on it. Every time I

The Filigree Cross

start the truck I offer up a prayer that it will haul this camping trailer to the next stop. Both vehicles are running on borrowed time."

Larry wondered how long Patrick's prayers could support the weight of that flat-bed on the car's shockless rear end.

Finished with the washing up, Patrick wiped the steel sink which was not much larger than a bowl, then he clipped the towel to a wire strung between cabinets to dry. He turned to Larry, rubbing his damp hands on his shirt front. "We'll put an air mattress on the flatbed for you, with a blanket. Will that be okay for sleeping tonight?"

SOMETHING ALWAYS NEEDED FIXING or cleaning or moving. Larry was kept so busy he couldn't imagine what they'd ever done without him. He fell asleep almost as soon as his head was down, right after he convinced himself that he could get through one more night without a drink.

At five o'clock Sunday afternoon, two burly men drove up to help lower the tent. Larry, Patrick, and Fiona had already collapsed the stage, an ingenious device consisting of interlocking two-by-sixes which required no tools or other materials for assembly.

"Who designed this?" Larry asked Patrick.

"I don't know. Clever, isn't it? I bought it from another preacher."

The men piled the boards on the flatbed. On top went three crates, with the folding chairs fitting perfectly inside.

When it came time to take the tent down Patrick asked Larry to simply watch. "There's a precise system for getting this tent to the ground, and since these fellows put it up, they know what needs to be done first."

The men disengaged the four main corner props, then, working evenly—going from side to side—dozens of wall braces came down. A huge skirt of green and white stripes lay on the ground pierced, tepee-like, by the center pole. Under that drape Larry could see the moving shape of one of the fellows from town. He must have been loosening the hawsers that balanced the pole because it slowly began to tip in one direction, then fell over on its side. The man crawled from under the edge of the tarp and stood up, sweating. Patrick handed him a glass of water.

He waved at Larry. "Now you can help."

Section by section, the four men dragged the heavy canvas and folded it over the fallen pole, finally lashing it into one unit. Larry's arms ached and he sucked air in great gulps, wishing that the man who so cleverly designed the stage had also created the tent. Then, two men to an end, they hoisted the pole, with its bulky wrapping, on to the crates of chairs and tied everything down.

Larry fell to the ground. "Jesus!" he exclaimed.

Then he saw Patrick's shoes beside him. He looked up. "Sorry. But what do you do when you only have three men?"

"Gillian makes the fourth."

"I can't believe it. It's too tough."

Patrick smiled across the wheat field. The sun was low, gilding his face. "She makes miracles; I told you."

Gillian and Fiona drove up, Gillian expertly backing the car to line up with the hitch on the flatbed.

The Filigree Cross

They had two plastic bags full of clean laundry in the back seat.

By seven-thirty camp was broken and they were ready to go.

Patrick tossed Larry the keys to the Oldsmobile.

This was the point of no return. All three of them watched his face. He tossed the keys in the air a couple of times then walked to the car.

Fiona sat beside him, nodding and bouncing to the radio, as they followed the hump-backed trailer down the highway. Before ten o'clock Patrick pulled into the driveway of a motel.

"Great!" Fiona shouted. "Real beds." She was out the door before the Oldsmobile had fully stopped, chasing her father into the office.

Larry walked over to Gillian's side of the truck. "This is a surprise," he said.

"It's in your honor. We seldom treat ourselves, but Patrick and I agreed that you deserved something for all your work this week."

"Well, Fiona's happy about it."

"She'll be up all night watching TV or listening to the radio, and she'll sleep all day tomorrow."

Gillian reached into the glove compartment and pulled out a leather change purse. She carefully unfolded one bill and handed Larry twenty dollars. "For a change of clothes. Take the car in the morning and see what you can find."

Larry hesitated. He deserved to be paid, and a lot more than twenty dollars, but this was their grocery and gas money.

Gillian smiled. "Come on, take it. You'll know it when we're *really* broke."

LARRY HADN'T REALIZED how much he missed his solitude. For four days he hadn't had one waking moment to himself. After a badly-needed shower, he stretched out on the bed naked. But he relaxed for only a moment before the thought of the twenty dollar bill began nagging at him. He could feel the soft curl of it in his hand when Gillian gave it to him and immediately that translated into the taste of what it could buy. Within a minute he was dressed and out the door.

He walked down the highway toward the center of town. He expected the clothing shops, the barber, and the hardware store to be closed, but even the small convenience store was dark. Then he remembered it was Sunday. Panic ran through him. Nothing would be open in this part of the country on a Sunday night. A sickening panic rose in his gut, doubling at the realization that inaccessibility could make his knees weak.

He began to jog, desperation rising, his eyes searching the side streets. He found a cab. A street lamp showed its driver, in shadow, asleep behind the wheel. Larry knocked on the glass. The man begrudgingly woke and rolled down the window.

Larry tried to put on a friendly smile. "I don't suppose you know where a guy can get a drink? Been on the road all day."

The man moved nothing but his eyes, surprisingly quick in the heavy body. He assessed Larry for a full minute. His face registered nothing.

"Where you from?"

"Down the road a bit."

The Filigree Cross

"Got friends here?"

Larry shook his head.

"Staying in town long?" The man hadn't moved a muscle in his upper body or his thick arms. Only those sharp eyes roamed over Larry's miserably dirty clothes. Larry wished he'd removed his crushed hat, but it was too late. He refrained from rubbing his hand over his mouth, which felt as dry as hell.

"We'll be on our way in the morning. Just passing through," he explained.

The big body seemed to sink, maybe relax, just a hair. One meaty hand moved to the top of the steering wheel. "There's a pool hall a few blocks down." He jerked his head backward to indicate it was behind him. "Go in from the alley. Say hi from Scotty."

Larry smiled his thanks and moved quickly. He had learned to shoot some mean pool in his travels. He could grow the twenty into forty or fifty easily.

The first couple of hours he held his own with a couple of guys who claimed to be the best in town. However, having gone almost a week without a drink, he put the cool beers away more quickly than was smart. First his concentration went, followed quickly by the thirty-five dollar profit he'd accumulated. Realizing he was in no shape to play, he moved to the bar and spent the last of his money on whiskey. When all the others had gone, the bartender said he needed to close up for a couple of hours of sleep.

Larry walked aimlessly for a few blocks, then, suddenly exhausted, sat hard on the curb, cursing his luck. He recalled a half dozen bad pool shots. Damn, should have taken my time, he muttered. His head fell between his knees. The next thing he knew he was being tapped in the side by a heavy boot. Now prone on the sidewalk, and cold, he squinted up the long length of a cop, the sky lightening behind him.

"Move along, mister," he said. "Your lucky day. Don't want to be bothered hauling you in this morning."

The cop watched as Larry slowly rose, attempting to keep his body in control and not stagger. He didn't remember which direction he had come from. But it hardly mattered whether he found the motel, he could not face the Brannigans anyway. He started walking in the opposite direction the cop had gone, looking for the bus depot.

Asleep once again, on a bench in the bus station, he was wakened this time by Patrick roughly shaking his shoulder.

"Get up, son," he said.

Larry stayed down. "I'm taking the bus."

"No, son. Get up. Gillie's in the car outside, waiting. Go get yourself washed up. You smell worse than the gutter."

Larry pushed himself to a sitting position, rubbing his face. He didn't have money for the bus. He had planned on begging a short lift or simply waiting until the Brannigans had moved on and try to earn a few dollars. But here was Patrick, ready to take him in again.

Larry went to the rest room and did his best to become presentable, but he still looked like a derelict as they approached the car. Larry crawled into the back seat; he couldn't look at Gillian. He studied the worn mat at his feet.

The Filigree Cross

Gillian's voice was like frost-bitten steel. "Fiona is too tired to drive this morning. You look too sick to drive. That means Patrick and I are going to have a very long day. Do you think that's fair, Larry?"

He shook his head, which throbbed.

"If we can't count on you, we don't need you."

Larry saw Patrick reach across the front seat and touch her hand as if to tell her to go easy. She ignored him.

"If you come with us now, this can never happen again. Never."

Larry began to tremble. "I've tried to stop. I can't."

"I don't believe you. But if you believe it, you'd better get out." She twisted around in her seat, reached over and opened the back door, letting it swing wide. The Oldsmobile rocked. A minute or two passed; then Larry stretched out and pulled the door shut.

BACK ON THE ROAD he sat in the truck beside Patrick, staring at the highway rolling under them, his body tense.

"Why don't you get some rest?" Patrick asked. "Then you can spell Gillie after a while."

"How come you're not hollering at me?"

"Would it help?"

"It would make me feel better."

"I think you're doing a pretty good job of hollering at yourself. But Gillie's serious. Never again. She'll kick you out as quick as she took you in, and for your own good."

Larry took a long swallow from the water jug. A slight dizziness spread through his brain, then settled down. "It's hotter 'n hell," he said.

"Not likely," Patrick answered, with a smile.

THE HEAT INTENSIFIED IN AUGUST. The odd thunder storm teased them, never doing much but making a lot of noise and settling the dust. Larry was driving with Gillian in the car, following the trailer, when the skies suddenly opened, dumping hail the size of a person's thumbnail. Immediately Patrick pulled the truck under the shelter of trees at the side of the road, and Larry tucked under some others. The hail fell so thickly he could barely see the outline of the truck only a few hundred feet ahead.

A flurry of stones smacked the windshield. Gillian jumped back at the sound, involuntarily sheltering her face with one hand.

"A few more like that, and we'll be driving in wind," she murmured.

Larry reached into the back seat and grabbed a blanket, planning to throw it across the outside of the glass, but the pattern of the hail changed abruptly. The stones made occasional dull thuds for a few moments, then dissipated into disjointed pops, decreasing in number and in strength.

Fiona came running toward them, her slim legs pumping with youth. Gillian rolled down her window.

"Wasn't that great!" Fiona poked her wet face inside the car. Damp tendrils of hair plastered her rosy cheeks.

"Surely you weren't standing outside?" her mother scolded.

"It was wonderful." She stood up straight, arms outstretched, and spun in a circle. "After all that heat."

The Filigree Cross

Her bra was outlined under her wet blouse, and Larry looked away, reminding himself of her age. Anyway, it was like watching a wood-nymph. Fiona exuded too much innocence for sex; too much sheer happiness for maturity.

But Larry knew that if he stayed with them and watched Fiona grow into womanhood, he would fall in love with her. He had never thought in terms of a permanent relationship, and that is what it would have to be with Fiona. It would mean life within the confines of this little church.

Patrick honked the horn, and Fiona ran back to the truck. Larry tried to concentrate on her lanky awkwardness and her childish, bouncing pony tail.

They rejoined the highway traffic. Streaks of sunlight glinted off small ice piles, slick pavement, and glossy leaves. But, too soon, steam rose from the hot road.

"I'm glad the storm's passing. We always enjoy setting up in Peoria," Gillian said, clicking on the radio. Larry paid no attention to the stations as she moved through them until Gillian stopped, her hand on the knob, and listened intently. Larry heard a unique, commanding voice.

"We invite all our old friends and all our new ones to the fall revival in Peoria, startin' tonight and continuin' for three weeks. Remember to look for the zeppelin!"

"Darn!" Gillian said, snapping off the radio.

"What's the matter?"

"That was J. Arnold Salsbury. He heads a giant revivalist and faith-healing church, and we're in their territory on their opening night."

"The competition?" Larry asked.

"We might as well not even set up. Everyone within fifty miles will be there. He puts on quite a show." She pointed to the truck ahead. "Blink at Patrick, will you?"

Larry flashed his headlights, and Patrick pulled over.

Patrick was more than disappointed, and agreed that it was useless to expect any kind of a turnout, even if they stayed several days. They decided to spend the night at a campground and move on in the morning.

THEY SET UP THE FOLDING TABLE between the truck and the car, a cozy situation made more pleasant by the smells of barbecue. But Patrick turned the hamburgers on the grill over and over, instead of letting them cook. Larry sat on a camp stool. Curly shavings piled at his feet as he carved a goose about six inches high. He was having trouble with the angle of the neck, and kept slicing peels so thin you could almost see through them.

"How'd you get so good at whittling?" Patrick asked.

"I started it at the Madison home. It's very calming, something I could do by myself. I liked that. I guess that's why I'm always copying the animals that lived there."

Patrick flipped a burger with a little too much energy, and it fell through the grill, onto the coals. He grumbled aloud, making more of it than the accident deserved.

"What's bugging you?" Larry asked.

The Filigree Cross

"Oh, I just hate to be driven out of town by the likes of Salsbury," Patrick said.

Gillian came out of the camper loaded down with a table cloth, napkins, and condiments. Larry helped her set the table.

"What's he like, Salsbury?" Larry asked.

Patrick huffed, like a disgruntled animal. "I say he survives on the two f's: frenzy and falsehood. He's one of those who makes a bad name for the rest of us on the road."

Fiona stuck her head out of the trailer. "You want to go see him?" she asked Larry.

She glanced at her mother and father, eyebrows raised. "It wouldn't hurt, would it?"

"It's a waste of time," Patrick put in, "and I hate to think that one of us would fill a seat in that miserable tent."

In the ensuing silence, Larry looked at Gillian. "I really would like to see one of these guys in action. I could go alone, if you'll lend me the car."

Fiona jumped down from the trailer. "Oh, Mom, can't I go? It'll be like a movie or something." She turned to her dad. "Daddy, let me go. I promise not to say a word or even whisper anything like a prayer."

Patrick spread the patties on the buns Gillian had prepared. He looked at his daughter and melted. "Well, you work so hard," he said. "And you never have friends around you in the summer. You can go if it's that important. But I don't want to hear one single word spoken about it afterwards."

CHAPTER SEVEN

"WHY ARE YOU SO GRUMPY?" Fiona asked. "You wanted to see him."

"If this Salsbury is so well known, you'd think the city would have been prepared for this heavy traffic and made some arrangements." Larry could see fifty or more cars ahead of him, all crawling slowly along the shoulder of the highway, the line lengthening behind them every minute. The sun bumped the horizon before it was finally their turn to pull off into a gravel road. Not much more than a rutted path, it dipped, then rose, and they could see into a shallow valley.

"Look at the size of that tent," Fiona exclaimed.

Larry couldn't even reply. He was so accustomed to the Brannigan's tent that the size of Salsbury's overwhelmed him. As they inched along, he could see it was more than a hundred feet wide on one side, its center rising almost two stories. Gigantic stretches of pale blue canvas spanned dozens of braces, a triangular white flag flying at the pinnacle of each brace. People swarmed between the large tent and a smaller one nearby, moving among merchandising booths. The scene resembled a medieval gathering from one of

The Filigree Cross

Larry's childhood books. He half expected knights in coats of mail to charge out on their steeds.

A young man waved, directing them into the parking area. It was a leveled field with roped pathways leading to the main entrance. The parking lot was edged by a line of massive trucks and travel trailers, which no doubt carried this spectacle across the country. As if the disappearing sun were a signal, the storm returned. Once outside the car, wind whipped at their legs, and Fiona pulled her jacket tighter.

Inside the main tent, people thronged—smiling, talkative, expectant. Some were well-dressed and some barely dressed, with all ages of children in tow. Lively organ music, played on stage by a man with a shock of white hair, could barely be heard over the noise of the crowd.

Fiona couldn't stop pointing and exclaiming about the lighting, the stage, the instruments. Larry listened to her with one ear. Many thoughts rolled around in his head, but uppermost was that he was witnessing a money-making machine. The tables lining the walls of this tent did not hold free peanut butter and ham sandwiches. They were stacked with several different books written by Salsbury, as well as calendars, notepads, shopping bags, school lunch boxes, all imprinted with the church's logo—"Miracles of Faith." Larry noticed magazine subscription forms for a bi-monthly publication produced by the church. Sales were brisk. The men and women who manned the cash boxes all wore dark blue vests and practiced, humble smiles.

Larry counted a hundred chairs, then counted twenty clumps of chairs about that size. The tent held approximately two thousand.

He and Fiona found seats three-quarters of the way back from the stage. "Oh, these are padded," Fiona said, settling into hers.

It took another fifteen minutes for the remaining seats to fill up. Precisely at eight-thirty the organ player took charge, raising the volume and the crowd settled down.

A familiar hymn, sung by a man, started softly offstage then swelled out from the loudspeakers. The lights over the audience dimmed, the ones on the stage brightened, and the singer appeared. Large and black, with an impressive stage presence, he moved slowly, capturing every eye. He sang with devotion and reverence, thoroughly quieting the crowd.

Behind him the musicians filed to their instruments. The band started all together on some invisible cue, utter professionals.

"Oh, I wish we could afford some musicians," Fiona sighed.

As the last musical notes faded, a middle-aged man replaced the singer, stepping up to the main microphone. He raised his arms and bent his head, inviting everyone to pray. He spoke in a flowing, vibrant voice, asking God to help them recognize their sins, begging God for forgiveness, promising God better behavior. His prayer went on so long that Larry heard much shifting in the audience, with parents trying to hush bored children.

After the prayer the man made a speech, welcoming everyone, a few by name, some by church

The Filigree Cross

denomination. He was attractive, with a commanding voice, but Larry couldn't believe all these trappings were supported by a man with so little charisma.

He whispered to Fiona. "I'm a little disappointed in him."

Grinning, she leaned over and put her mouth to his ear. "This is only the front man, silly."

Soon Larry realized why Fiona had found his comment so entertaining.

When Salsbury strutted out, the crowd went mad. All eyes strained toward the stage. Men stood, holding children on their shoulders, and women climbed on chairs. Between waving arms and clapping hands, Larry spotted the evangelist roaming the stage, smiling and banging a tambourine on his hip. He was in his sixties, paunchy, and wore a baby blue suit, pink shirt, and a vest beneath his unbuttoned jacket, which flew open like a cape.

The din was deafening, yet Salsbury's voice rose above it. "Does anybody out there know how to shout Amen?"

A thousand Amens filled the tent.

"Do you think our Lord *heard* that?"

The Amens were shouted again, twice as loud.

"Well, maybe he heard *that* one," Salsbury said. He raised the tambourine and shook it violently. His voice strained to a high pitch. "And maybe He's sayin' welcome and maybe He's sayin' thanks for comin', and maybe He's saying you're going to see some *miracles* here tonight!"

Bedlam. Fiona clapped her hands over her ears. She turned to Larry and giggled, though he couldn't hear it. She shouted at him, "See? It's just like a movie."

Larry heard nothing from the stage for a few moments and realized Salsbury was waiting for everyone to calm down. Slowly people began to sit, with much adjusting of clothing and muttering of blessings.

The evangelist stood perfectly still, confident quiet would prevail. Larry could now see his fancy cowboy boots, polished to a high sheen. The man gazed out over the crowd, pleased. He spoke softly, so they had to concentrate to catch his words.

"I'm so glad you all could come tonight." A murmur began to grow in the audience, but he held up his hand for continued quiet.

"We've been on the road for a week, aimin' for Peoria. Our eyes on the road, looking for Peoria, anxious to see all our friends again. I knew you wouldn't disappoint us." He half turned to look downstage. "Counting these dozen talented musicians behind me, there's thirty-one of us who work daily to bring God's word and healing to you. Some are wives, some are children. We travel all year long spreading God's message of hope for the infirm, and God's promise of everlasting life for the faithful, and God's protection through the practice of baptism. We will hold a baptism at the end of our three-week stay, out at the lake, as usual, and hope to bring hundreds of new souls into our Savior's care. Please visit us many times over the next three weeks, and bring your friends."

He bowed his head and began a prayer. "Dear God, we thank You tonight for bringing all these wonderful people out in such a ragin' storm. It only proves the

The Filigree Cross

strength of their desire to witness for themselves Your wonderful healing powers, and I know You will meet their every expectation, and exceed many."

Salsbury preached for over an hour, controlling his momentum so that at no time did the sermon seem long. Larry heard nothing new. Salsbury talked about the same things as Patrick did—salvation, devotion, the wages of sin—but he and Patrick didn't speak the same language. Salsbury made it all sound like a game, exciting and enticing. He played shamelessly on people's emotions, ignoring common sense.

He began to wind down, looking a little weary, speaking more slowly.

"And now, we need to tell God that this church is valuable to you. We need to show Him that we will keep this ministry before the people, a ministry open to every denomination, every color, every level of prosperity, every*body*."

People, knowing what was to come, began digging into pockets and purses. Several men in blue vests walked to the heads of the aisles, carrying galvanized cans the size of garbage pails. No felt-lined fishbowls here.

People rose, shuffled down the rows of seats to the aisles and filed past the cans, depositing donations. Larry heard very little clanking of change, and by the time he and Fiona approached their collector, he could see the can was half full of bills. Fiona dropped in a quarter, and Larry stuck his hand in, pretending to leave paper money. The man holding the container was not fooled and made a point of saying, "God bless you."

A small choir had formed on stage, a few men and women dressed in simple smocks. They sang softly while the collection was taking place. Salsbury did not leave the stage, but stood alone, head down, as if in prayer. The lines of bodies wound their way back to their seats. Salsbury rose and blessed them all for their generosity. Then he left the stage to the musicians. The black man whom they'd seen earlier, led the congregation in several hymns, the words to which were on flyers that had been placed on the seats.

Toward the end of "The Old Rugged Cross," Salsbury reappeared, without his jacket and tie, singing in a strong, clear voice. At the end of the hymn, he draped the microphone cord around his neck, picked up the tambourine, and began to strut, banging the instrument alternately against his hip and his palm. The musicians followed his lead, moving into a solid beat that set feet to tapping.

Larry sensed anticipation in the crowd. Necks were being craned to get a better look at the stage.

"Are we ready?" Salsbury shouted.

"Yes!"

"Are we ready for God's miracles?" The music built constantly, threatening to overcome his voice.

"Yes!"

"Can you say, Praise the Lord?"

"Praise the Lord!"

"Let Him hear it!"

"Praise the Lord!"

The cadence grew, drowning out the musicians. Larry wondered just how much noise everyone could stand.

The Filigree Cross

As the clapping and stamping and shouting continued, Salsbury descended the steps and began to help people onstage. A half dozen young men accompanied him, and soon it was half-filled with people bearing canes, leaning on crutches, sitting in wheelchairs, even one prone on a stretcher.

Salsbury spoke to each one privately for just a few seconds, the microphone held behind his back. Then he retraced his steps and approached a woman on crutches. She was grossly overweight, and Larry could almost feel the pain in her arms as she supported more than two hundred pounds of fat. The music stopped. The crowd was seated, but restless.

"Muriel," Salsbury said. "God is here with us today. He wants you to be well. Do you believe that God wants you to be well?" He stuck the microphone in her face.

The woman nodded vehemently, tears streaking her round cheeks.

"Say it, Muriel."

"God wants me to be well." She was crying so hard she could barely speak.

"I don't think they heard you."

She spoke up. "God wants me to be well."

"Do you have enough faith in Him that you can accept a miracle?"

The poor woman was sobbing, shaking all over.

"Do you, Muriel? Have enough faith?" Clearly, Larry thought, if the healing failed, it would not be the fault of the evangelist, or God.

"Yes!" Muriel shouted. "I love God!"

Salsbury put his right palm on her forehead, raised his head toward the ceiling, and prayed. "Dear Lord, show Muriel that her faith is rewarded. Bless her with Your love, and healing."

Then he finished very quickly, saying, "Bless and heal Muriel today." He seemed to push very slightly on her forehead, in the same instant retracting his hand. Muriel burst into a radiant smile, shoved her crutches away, and fell backward. A whoosh of drawn-in breaths rose from the congregation, but waiting arms of several men caught her. They lifted her back on her feet. She balanced there, then triumphantly raised her hands in the air.

"Thank you, God," she cried.

Breathy Amens rose from the audience.

Salsbury moved quickly along the lines of the hopeful, alternately beseeching the Lord and giving thanks. Occasionally he touched a forehead with much the same response as he'd gotten from Muriel. People were fainting away and being propped back up like dominoes. With each miracle the congregation became more frenzied.

Larry's eyes sought out poor Muriel again. She was no longer standing, but sitting on stage in a folding chair. Still, she raised her arms and voice in gratitude.

Salsbury moved to the man on the stretcher. This time he didn't exhort the crowd, but used the quiet to enhance suspense. He leaned over, apparently praying with the invalid. Slowly Salsbury straightened, raising his fully-extended arms. Like a puppet attached to Salsbury's fingers, the man rose on his elbows, then braced himself with his hands. He grimaced as one thin leg slid over the side of the stretcher, and he sat up. He looked like a ghost, his skin as pale as the hospital gown he wore.

The Filigree Cross

"More, God. More." Salsbury implored.

The man gripped the edge of the stretcher and stood. He wavered; Larry heard breaths being sucked in. Salsbury didn't move. Neither did any of the men who had braced Muriel and the others. Larry wondered how they knew that this person was not going to fall over.

As the pale man moved feebly backstage, Salsbury turned to the crowd, shouting, "Is the Lord here with us?"

The congregation erupted.

Salsbury shouted over them. "Has God shown his love for us?"

"Yes!"

"God wants us all to be well in spirit *and* in body. Only our lack of faith can keep us from being complete in both body and soul."

Larry squirmed in his seat. Patrick would never allow people to blame themselves for unavoidable illnesses. Salsbury was saying that only the faithless suffered from tuberculosis or cancer.

"How many of us have a faith so complete that it conquers every inspiration of the devil? So complete that we can call on God and be sure of his intervention? If your own faith is lacking, if you are strugglin', if you don't believe He will come to you in your hour of need, then you must give more of yourself to God. And one of the ways to show God that you are devoted and trying is to support this church."

Larry couldn't believe the man's blatant transition from spirituality to money. Only he and Fiona seemed to register any skepticism as Salsbury launched directly into a brazen attempt to extort more donations.

He told of the church's visit to Africa the previous year.

"We saw people living in conditions where we not keep our dogs." He drew it out long—dawgs. "These poor people gave freely of the little they had. One woman offered a basket holding a piece of elephant tusk or some kind of horn. I didn't understand its significance, but someone explained that it was a precious possession, and she gave it willingly.

"Could you bring something in *your* basket that would really *mean* something to the Lord? If a rich man gives two thousand dollars, is he giving something that means anything? No. But if a poor man gives twenty dollars, now that *means* something."

Larry quickly calculated twenty dollars times two thousand poor men. Forty thousand.

"God would rather have twenty dollars given out of devotion and self-sacrifice than a million dollars given for show. And remember, there are rewards for our generosity. Our deeds are weighed in Heaven. If you don't know how much you should give, ask Jesus. If He says to give more than you have, then make a covenant. Promise the amount you *want* to give. Promise it in your heart and He will show you a way to get that money.

"Now I'm going to ask Gerald and his helpers to pass the plates." A general scuffling ensued. "If you don't have anything to give, please write your covenant on a scrap of paper. Tell God you will give that as soon as you can, and He will help you. Maybe He'll show you the way to a new job. Maybe He'll bring you more fortune than you can even dream of. It has happened. It can happen again."

The Filigree Cross

Larry thought Salsbury knew of what he spoke.

Salsbury continued in this same vein as shallow plates were passed down the rows. Quickly filled, they were replaced by empty ones. Not too many people put covenants on slips of paper; the donations were obvious to neighbors.

Music swelled, then slowed. The men with the plates disappeared. Salsbury stood center stage, mike in hand, sweating profusely. He looked physically and psychologically drained, as if, by emptying their pockets, the people had finally sapped all the man's energy. He raised his hand and gave a short Benediction. The audience, now equally exhausted, bowed their heads. Salsbury thanked them again for coming and reminded them about their three-week stay and the baptism.

"Come again, and bring your friends and neighbors," he urged before leaving the stage.

People stood slowly, stretching, gathering their things and their sleeping children. Larry looked over them, toward the infirm who were being helped from the stage. Although a few did seem to move a little more easily, most were unchanged. Muriel, her face streaked with tears, was being supported by burly men, one on either side. Below the stage waited another man, perhaps her husband, holding out her crutches.

Fiona stood and pushed her arms overhead in a full stretch. Larry was unable to ignore the slim line of her waist. As her jacket rode up, an inch of bare skin showed above her slacks.

"Wow," she said, dropping her arms and smiling down at him. "That was worth the money."

Marlene Baird

But for the first time that evening, Larry wasn't thinking about money.

CHAPTER EIGHT

"TERRE HAUTE?" PATRICK RAISED HIS eyes from the map and invited comments.

Larry shrugged. He wouldn't know Terre Haute from Denver.

They all looked at Gillian. "That's fine with me, if we can stay at the same campground. It's near the bus stop, for Fiona."

They were huddled, knees bumping, in the humid trailer while a slashing rain pelted the metal shell. Here was togetherness in all its stickiness, Larry thought.

Fiona was pleased. They had apparently stayed the winter in Terre Haute two years ago. If she could go to the same school maybe the kids would remember her.

And so, with a few words, their winter domicile was decided.

Larry didn't know why it bothered him, now, to see the three of them content with so little, but suddenly it angered him. Why didn't they spend winters in a better climate? While they had been moving about the country there had seemed to be a sense of adventure about them. Now he saw three people controlled by circumstance, without a plan. He imagined himself wintering in Florida or California, but every picture of sun and sea included Fiona. He realized he was waiting for her to grow up and run away with him. And if she was foolish enough to do that, what could he offer her? But how difficult could it be to do better than what she had now?

Meanwhile, with winter coming, and no moving from place to place, no tent to raise or errands to run, the little circle would choke him. Either that or he would turn to old habits.

THEY HAD BEEN AT THE CAMPGROUND for a few days when Larry found Patrick alone in the trailer. The women were shopping for Fiona's school clothes. Patrick, Bible in hand, looked completely at home; in fact all three of them had settled down within hours, planting themselves as easily as they'd uprooted themselves all summer.

"How are jobs around here?" Larry asked.

Patrick put down his reading. "Good. We can always find something pretty quickly. You going job hunting?"

Larry nodded.

Patrick sighed. "I was going to set up the tent for a week or two, but with this weather..."

Gusty rainstorms had been incessant. "Surely it will get nice again before winter sets in," Larry said hopefully.

"Probably. But we can't go too long without some money coming in. I guess I'll head down to the hardware store and see if they remember me."

"Is there a supermarket near here?" Larry asked. "I guess I'd qualify for stocking shelves."

The Filigree Cross

Patrick encouraged him to set his sights a bit higher. "Remember, I'll give you a heck of a recommendation."

Larry started two weeks later at a stationery firm, stocking and delivering. He found a room in a boarding house and visited the Brannigans two or three times a week, always hoping to see Fiona. Too often he was disappointed; she had thrown herself into every school activity available, and flitted through their lives.

The winter was milder than Larry expected, but still dragged. Almost weekly he could see Patrick aging. As spring approached and Patrick saw the end of Fiona's school year, Larry watched him become more and more eager to get moving.

"I can barely stand not to be preaching," he explained one evening. Larry had found him giving the flatbed a coat of paint. Gillian and Fiona had gone to a movie. "Winters are interminable for me." He held up his paint brush. "What do you think about this color?"

"They say red is the safest color on the highway, can be seen the best."

"Well, they'll see us coming this year," Patrick beamed. "Gillian said we can trade in the car or the truck, my choice. What do you think? What's worse, transmission problems or ignition problems?" He laughed, spreading a thick line of red on the old wood. He had apparently forgotten about having to fix the broken axle and both muffler jobs.

Larry couldn't concentrate on Patrick's dilemma. He was trying to visualize the three of them back on the road without him.

"I really like my job, Patrick. They've been good to me."

Patrick stopped painting. He kept his back to Larry, standing still. Slowly he turned, forcing a smile. "Are you saying you want to stay, son? Because we'd never hold you back. You know that."

It was hard for Larry to swallow; his throat hurt.

"I don't know. I can't imagine not being out there with you." He took a deep breath. Patrick might hate his next idea, the one he'd lain awake all night pondering. He cleared his throat. "What about staying put, renting a meeting hall here in the city? You wouldn't need a new car, and I can contribute some money. We're all working."

Unable to face Patrick straight on, he paced beside the flatbed. Patrick said nothing.

Larry pressed on. "It's a pretty good sized city. Or maybe Indianapolis would be better?" He looked eagerly at Patrick.

Patrick put down his brush. "I'd hate not having you with us, Larry. But I love the moving around. New people, being out under God's sky. It's just better."

He clapped Larry on the back. "But don't worry about us. I'll hire more help so the ladies don't have to go back to being dray horses." His voice was rough and caught on the last few words. His eyes filled with tears and he looked down at his shoes.

"What's the matter?" Larry asked.

"Oh, Lord. It's so much more than the open sky and moving on." He raised his eyes, asking Larry to understand. "So much more, son. I think I'm afraid of standing still, as if something is going to catch up with me."

"Like what?"

The Filigree Cross

"Like my own failure. As long as I keep moving I can keep attracting a crowd, at the very least of the curious. But if I stop, can I sustain one?"

"Patrick, you're a fine preacher. When you speak people are locked on to you. They love the natural humility of your faith. Everyone responds to it."

Larry put an arm around Patrick's shoulder. He couldn't watch the man's pain. "If my plan doesn't work and you really want to go back on the road, I promise I'll come along for one more year. But, please, just try sitting still for a while."

"I know how much Gillian and Fiona would love it," Patrick conceded.

They discussed the pros and cons of staying, and when the ladies returned from the movies, put the suggestion to them. Fiona's shouts could be heard well beyond the campground.

"Oh, Dad," she exclaimed, throwing her arms around Patrick. "All the kids at school keep talking about going to Indiana U. I never could say a word, because I never knew where we'd be." She kissed him on the cheek with a smacking sound.

Larry watched her telling her parents all her big plans—plans she'd kept to herself up until now. She wanted to be a biologist, of all things.

Almost a year had passed since she'd nearly run him over. He saw the beautiful woman emerging and wondered how many of her new school friends were young men.

"Do we have money for college?" she asked suddenly.

Marlene Baird

Patrick's eyes fell gently on Gillian. "How can you doubt it? Your mother's been multiplying nickels and dimes for years, just waiting for this day."

BY THE TIME FIONA ENTERED her senior year of high school the Brannigans were living in a rented house, and the Church of God's Love had its own hall on an untidy street in Terre Haute. They held services three times a week, and more people came every month. Gillian still had sandwiches and coffee available in a small alcove off the main room, and Larry attended every service because that was almost the only time he could see Fiona.

She turned eighteen in August, the summer after high school, and was headed for college. He panicked whenever he thought of it. He had been waiting for her to grow up, and now she had. But how could he ever compete with the possibilities that college would open up for her? Still, he wanted her to know how he felt before she left.

On the last Sunday in August, Patrick cut the service short. The air was thick and muggy, and his congregation was struggling to pay attention.

Larry caught up to Fiona as she left the building, pulling her aside. "Can you come for a walk? We never get to talk anymore."

Gray clouds, just begging to drop rain, huddled over them. Larry's shirt stuck to his sides, but even in the humidity his throat was dry.

"I'll miss you," he said.

She smiled at him and took his hand. "I'll miss you, too. But I'm not going to be that far away."

The Filigree Cross

Larry withdrew his hand, and halted, forcing her to look at him. "No, Fiona. I mean, I love you. I've loved you for a long time."

Her brow creased as she searched his face. One palm went to his cheek, her thumb stroking his skin. It was their first intimate, physical contact, and the touch made Larry weak with desire. "Oh, Larry. I love you, too. But—" she added, breaking his heart.

He grabbed her hand, interrupting her. He wanted to wrap his arms around her, beg her to stay, but it was too unfair.

"I know you need to do this. You deserve to go away and experience all the wonderful things that await you. I'd never ask you to give that up."

"It's not forever."

But he knew it would be. His narrow, scraping life would seem silly after she saw the real world.

Then she stood on her toes, pulled his face down and kissed his eyelids. Her fingertips were as soft as an angel's wings. A gust of wind blew her hair across his face. He drew a deep breath so as not to forget its scent.

Two days later she packed up the Oldsmobile and headed for Indianapolis.

THE STORY UNFOLDED OVER TWO days in shocking, breath-suspending bits and pieces. Patrick, Gillian and Larry were in escalating anguish as horrifying details piled one upon another.

The Oldsmobile had broken down on the highway. A couple of witnesses, speeding by, thought they had seen a man helping a young woman. The police searched for half a day before they found her, near death, in Turkey Run Park. Her upper torso and right arm had been slashed repeatedly by a knife, her face disfigured. Investigation showed that she had been beaten and raped over a period of several hours.

They found the man the next day. The act had proven too gruesome even for him. He hung from a tree with his own bloody belt around his neck.

CHAPTER NINE

LARRY SAT AT THE TABLE in his room trying to compose a notice to tack up at the meeting hall. It was all he could do to hold the black marker in his hand. Grief now blanketed all their lives—a harsh, suffocating fabric, its hems weighted with lead. Larry dragged through the days in a gunky darkness peopled with whispering shadows. His nights had been stolen by a madman. He pummeled the man's face with his bare fists until he could no longer raise his arms, and still the taunting face haunted him.

He had nearly collapsed after his first visit to the hospital. All manner of technical devices beeped and blimped around Fiona's bed, assuring visitors that she was, in fact, alive, but there was no trace of her. Her face was discolored and swollen beyond recognition, and she radiated less life than a scarecrow. Her one good hand lay on the top of the sheet. Larry stroked it gently with a finger and felt a barely perceptible withdrawal, less than a flinch, which told him she was too weak to even complain.

Larry attempted, again, to devise a proper notice. Ten days had passed since Fiona's attack and, still, nothing worked properly, not even his fingers. His mind wandered to thoughts of her struggle, to her innocence. Having been raised like she was, so protected from the outside world, she must have thought—Lord, what must she have thought? Was she conscious through it all? How long did she fight? He remembered the melting softness of her hands and wrists and knew they would have been feathers against the brute's strength.

He clutched the marker like a weapon and stabbed the cardboard over and over, cursing. His body began to shake. He thought of the relief he knew he could count on—booze. He closed his eyes and squeezed the pen in his fist; it became a crumpled beer can, cold and sharp-edged. Saliva burst from beneath his tongue. Larry leaped from his chair, shoving the table with his thighs. He paced the room. *Later. Not now. But later.* Gillian had asked one small favor of him. Just make a notice to tack on the door of the meeting hall. If nothing else, he could do this one constructive thing.

"What shall I say?" he had asked her.

"Promise something," she mumbled. Her eyes, dark holes in a furiously lined face, pleaded with him. "Patrick must have something to go back to when he's ready."

Larry threw away the piece of poster board he had ruined and began another. The attack had made headlines, so most of the congregation would be aware of the situation, but he needed to let them know that Patrick would be back. No earlier than a month, he guessed. But what if Patrick rallied before then, wanted to preach, and no one came? Unable to come to a decision about what to say, Larry decided to go down

The Filigree Cross

and talk to whoever showed up at the hall the next evening.

WHEN HE DROVE UP THE SIDE street, he couldn't believe his eyes. Well over a hundred people stood waiting outside. They bore flowers, food, wrapped gifts, and someone had hung a lovely arch of greenery over the entrance.

Larry unlocked the door, and they followed him inside. Quietly, they put their gifts on the side table and took seats. Larry had no choice but to move to the front of the hall. He sat on the edge of the stage. A few heads were bent in silent prayer, but most people seemed to be looking to him for guidance.

He looked at the floor and cleared his throat. "I guess you'd like to have some news."

Nods and hopeful half-smiles greeted this.

"I know there has been some rumor that Fiona died." He had to gulp air; the sound of her name almost dissolved him. "She is alive. Just."

Sympathetic sighs rose from the crowd. He drew a long, deep breath. "She is in deep shock from severe trauma. The doctors do not promise good results. At least for a long time."

Actually the prognosis was even worse than that, and Larry found that talking about it helped him to grasp the facts himself. Fiona was now a stranger to them all, no longer anyone they knew. He gazed around the hall, taking in the corners. Surely her soul, her sweet goodness, must still exist, somewhere.

Larry paused in his discourse as his mind wandered. Then a man in the audience said, "Shall we pray?" Larry jerked out of his reverie. "Of course."

Marlene Baird

After an awkward delay, Larry bent his head and began. The words came naturally. They weren't Patrick's words, though Larry knew those by heart. They were Larry's own. He pretended there was a God to listen, because these people expected that, and he could not deal with the tragedy alone.

"Dear God, be with Gillian and Patrick today as they try to reach their daughter." Amens rumbled. "And let Fiona come back to us. She loved You as the earth loves the rain; needed You as a baby bird needs food from its mother's mouth. She never doubted You, and would not doubt You now. Please, God, we are dull and slow to see, but find a way to help us understand."

When he stopped he felt the breathless quiet in the room. Then the hall seemed to utter a communal sigh.

Slowly, people cleared throats and sat upright. Women fumbled with purses and chairs scraped. It seemed to be over. A man approached Larry, gripping his forearm. "Thank you, son," he said.

GILLIAN AND PATRICK WERE out of their minds with guilt at having sent Fiona off in the old car. They spent most of their time at her bedside in the hospital, initially in the ICU, then in the mental ward. Larry had watched them beg Fiona for some sign of recognition. She only stared at them with steely eyes. Nothing penetrated her gaze, from outside or from within. One moment they thought she hated them; the next moment they feared she was lost to them forever, lost behind eyes that would tell them nothing. And when the bandages came off her jaw, neither did she speak. Nor touch, nor want to be touched.

The Filigree Cross

THE CHURCH HAD DEVELOPED a patterned following, each service attracting a different crowd. Sunday mornings brought more elderly; the weekday evenings more young people. Larry went to each scheduled meeting, talking, giving what little news there was, and praying with the congregation. The numbers dropped off, but not dramatically, as Larry constantly mentioned Patrick's return.

During the third week Gillian joined him, wanting people to know things would soon return to normal—if anything would ever be normal again. She'd aged ten years, her face hollow, shoulders stooped and collarbone sharp. But she put aside her pain and added her own prayers to Larry's, sounding more like Patrick, more biblical. She gave a message of hope even while she lived in despair, and the congregation responded to her courage.

The next Sunday morning she brought Fiona's guitar. Larry's heart cracked at hearing almost the same voice singing those simple hymns. The congregation quickly came to full voice, and a summit of grief seemed to have been reached. Smiles spread on a few faces, and eyes lifted and sparkled, as they began down the easier road.

When they were alone, Gillian turned to Larry. "You speak beautifully. I'm so proud."

Embarrassed, he felt heat run through his body. He shook his head and shrugged. "They're just simple prayers."

"That's what a lot of people need. Just simple prayers. Do they come easily to you?"

He nodded. Why they came, he couldn't imagine.

Marlene Baird

"Well, you have a gift. For all the years I've been at Patrick's side I still have to work at it. I struggle to recite his words, and I never have an original thought."

"But you sound as natural as he does."

"Can you imagine how many sermons I've heard him deliver? How many prayers he's said in the house? Thousands and thousands. Every hesitation, every intona-tion is embedded in my subconscious."

"Will he be back next week?"

"Yes. He promised. Wednesday night."

BUT PATRICK DIDN'T COME BACK on Wednesday. Nor did Gillian. Larry couldn't face anyone, either. The day they got the terrible news—that Fiona was pregnant—the three of them stared at the walls of the doctor's office, through windows, at the ceiling, anything to avoid eye contact. The doctor assured them the baby would be healthy, provided Fiona could be kept from injuring herself.

Larry went directly to the meeting hall. Making a wild guess, he tacked a scribbled notice on the door. *Rev. Patrick Brannigan will resume preaching October 15. We look forward to seeing you.* Then he bought armloads of beer and wine and left the world.

After three days of oblivion he woke to banging on his door and Patrick's voice. "Larry, are you ill? Open up."

"I'm okay," he shouted, his voice so thick the words were almost incoherent. There were a few moments of silence then he heard Patrick's steps moving away.

In the following days Larry waited for Patrick's censure, but Patrick just looked at him with heavy eyes

The Filigree Cross

and Larry cringed to know he had added to the man's distress.

On October fifteenth Patrick took the pulpit. His audience had dwindled to about half of what it had been, but they were attentive, anxious to reclaim him. For the first five or so minutes he seemed like his old self, reveling in the Lord's power to bring people together, where support multiplied tenfold. He read scripture, spoke of everyday struggles and God's pervading strength. Larry allowed his hands to unclench and saw Gillian, seated on the stage, relax into her chair.

Then Patrick took a different tack, and the hair on Larry's neck stood up. "God's will. What can we know of it? It is so grand, so all-encompassing, that it evades us in its magnitude. We need simply to trust; trust in His undying love for all. The weak, the forceful, the mean . . . even the cruel." His voice trailed off. Larry saw him biting at his lip. Then tears slipped down Patrick's cheeks. Patrick opened his mouth as if to speak, but dropped his chin to his chest. Larry looked to Gillian. She was faltering, too.

Larry jumped from his seat and took the stage. He bent into the microphone.

"We know healing is coming. We know God has not forgotten our sweet Fiona, nor Patrick and Gillian."

He stepped back between the two of them and took one hand of each in his own. He raised their interlocked fists into the air. Patrick's hand shook, and Gillian sobbed aloud. Larry looked heavenward, then pleaded. "God, look at us here. Send Your healing breath. Touch us with Your caring hands. Forgive us our doubts. We don't know Your plan; we're blinded by our own fears. Take off our blinders, God. Shine understanding into our hearts."

They stood very still, arms upraised, and Larry, eyes closed, thought he felt a surge passing through him from Patrick to Gillian. She turned her head and mimed the words, "Thank you."

A man with a rich baritone voice began to hum "Amazing Grace, how sweet the sound." Slowly others joined in. The beautiful tune swirled around them until the entire hall was filled with it. Larry felt as if he were buoyant in warm water. People linked hands and began to sway. Larry, Patrick, and Gillian did the same, and Gillian began to sing. Her lovely soprano rose above the other voices, a crippled dove soaring, finally breaking out of its cage of pain.

The Filigree Cross

PART THREE

1998

Jericho

Marlene Baird

CHAPTER TEN

LARRY ROSE FROM HIS DESK, rubbing cramped muscles in his neck and arms. Twenty-six years. Twenty-six years since that moment of healing at the October service, when Patrick, Gillian, and he had been released from the depths of pure despair. An infant had made it possible for them to continue. Fiona's baby, Sue, shunned by her mother, became their anchor. A serene baby, solidly built, her facial expression neither gay nor solemn, she studied the world through dark brown eyes with a gaze as steady as stone. Holding her, on the evenings when Patrick and Gillian took some time for themselves, Larry fed off her calm. She had none of Fiona's delicate beauty—but Fiona was in her, and, even then, Sue carried a dignity that transcended the mean reality of her conception.

Larry picked up a small carved duck that had been the paperweight on his desk for years. Stroking its smooth back with his thumb, he saw that when carving it he had captured something very fine in the convergence of the features. It seemed almost to speak, and its message was soothing. Perhaps it would be a good birthday present for Fiona.

HE TOOK SUE'S SQUARE HAND as they walked the hallway toward her mother's room. He rolled his shoulders, trying to loosen tight muscles and shake off the anxiety of seeing Fiona. She was now in Golden Hills, one of Chicago's finest clinics, but the best care money could buy hadn't been able to rehabilitate her.

In the early years Patrick and Gillian had bemoaned the fact that they couldn't afford the very best for her. But Dr. Freidman, her doctor and the medical administrator of Golden Hills, had reviewed her extensive files and said the state institutions probably had done as much for her as was possible.

For many years Fiona had suffered debilitating depression. No amount of counseling could break her will; she absolutely refused to speak of her attack. Early on, they had brought her home from the various clinics from time to time, until the second of her two suicide attempts. Thereafter, she was left in professional care where numbing doses of medication only served to help her retreat in a different way, and she made no progress.

Although not at present in a state of depression, nor on heavy medication, she was locked away in a fantasy world, her mind secluded in some safe place where ugliness couldn't reach her.

The clinic hallway seemed to stretch a mile. "Are we having a full rehearsal this afternoon?" Larry asked Sue. He needed to remind himself that this journey

The Filigree Cross

between stark walls was just a short break in his normal day.

"No. Just a run-through with our guest. She and Jimmy have had only a few minutes to practice. I'm not asking the entire orchestra or the full choir to come out."

Sue motioned toward the shopping bag in his hand.

"What have you brought? Cookies?"

"Of course. And a book that your grandmother suggested. Plus a carved duck. Do you think she'll like that?"

"Yes. I think she will."

"When were you here last?" Larry asked, feeling guilty about his own poor record of visits.

"I came with Grandma about two months ago. But Grandma came every week up until three weeks before she died."

"How much does it bother you to visit?"

"When I was young it was awful. Even though Grandma tried to explain, to prepare me, I still expected Mother to make some indication that she knew me."

Larry squeezed her hand in under-standing, prompting Sue to continue.

"As you know, in those early years her moods were unpredictable, you couldn't anticipate what kind of a reception you would get. Sometimes she would be angry and make us leave." She sighed. "After all this time I have found *some* peace. But I regret never knowing her like you all did. I've never known her when she was well."

"She was graceful and cheerful . . ." Larry's voice trailed off. It pained him to remember.

"I try to picture her as normal but it's impossible. I wish there were more photos of her."

"The family was on the road and dirt poor for most of Fiona's childhood. A camera and film would have been luxuries."

"It's hard to imagine that, when we have so much now."

"Yes, so much," Larry said. *Just not quite enough.*

Sue paused at a door decorated with a wild mass of daisies and pansies.

"This is hers?" Larry asked.

"She painted it one day. The staff have been good enough to leave it alone."

Larry opened the door and they stepped inside. Fiona looked up from where she sat on the floor. She was a flower herself, amid a garden of floral paintings taped to the walls. Someone had also taped up important newspaper stories. A picture of the moon landing was yellowed, and curled at the edges. Larry wondered how much of that accomplishment Fiona had been able to grasp.

She gave them a smile and put down the bottle of polish she was using to color her toenails.

Countless plastic surgeries had returned her to normal appearance. She carried only some scar tissue above and below her left eye and when she moved her facial muscles a certain way there was a very slight twitch beneath the skin of one cheek—irreparable nerve damage. But she was beautiful, and to Larry, breathtakingly so.

She pushed herself up and stood facing them, apparently glad for the company, but with no personal welcomes, even for Sue.

The Filigree Cross

"Hello, Fiona. Do you remember me?" Larry asked.

She cocked her head and may have nodded; it was impossible to be sure. He leaned down and kissed her lightly on the cheek. She rubbed at it and turned shy.

Sue said "Hello, Mother," sliding her hand down the long shaft of Fiona's auburn hair—the only thing about which Fiona seemed vain. "Your hair looks lovely today."

"How are you?" Larry asked, feeling totally inadequate himself.

Fiona studied his face. Though after a few moments Larry began to feel self-conscious, Fiona didn't register any discomfort as she merely looked at him. "I'm fine," she said, finally and sat back down on the floor.

Before she could return to her nail painting, Larry handed her the bag of gifts. She quickly unwrapped the book and ran her fingers over the glossy cover. She opened it, looking at several brightly colored reproductions, smiling. Then she dipped her hand back into the shopping bag, asking, "Did you bring cookies?"

Larry sat cross-legged beside her. She seemed amused at the effort it took him to fold his long legs. He had bought some oatmeal raisin cookies at the bakery and put them on one of Gillian's plates. He folded back the tin foil. She reached eagerly and chewed with enthusiasm. I must have guessed well, he thought. Or, more likely, she likes all cookies. Otherwise Gillian would have been more specific.

He took the duck from the bag and handed it to Fiona. "This is a birthday present from me. I made it."

Her eyes shone with admiration as she turned it over and over in her hands. "You made it?" Here was the essence of the young Fiona. Excitement and innocence.

Sue was walking around the room, apparently taking inventory.

"Are you looking for something?" Larry asked.

"No. Just making sure nothing has been stolen."

Fiona ignored their conversation, studying the duck.

"Surely that's not a worry here," Larry said to Sue.

"It happens once in a while."

One wall held shelves with the gifts Gillian had brought in the past six months. There was a standing arrangement with the clinic that the older gifts were to be given to charities unless it was something Fiona seemed to like. But Fiona's favorites were always the newest ones; she didn't bond to anything, or anyone.

Fiona set the duck carefully on the floor and opened the book at random. Her face lit, and she sighed. She touched Larry's sleeve. "Look at these angels."

Degas ballerinas floated in frothy dresses, stretching elegant arms. The walls behind them were splashed with blues and greens, and a brass rail caught a shaft of sun.

"They're dancers," Larry said.

"I know. They're dancing angels," Fiona replied.

She pushed herself up from the floor and began whirling around the room. As she spun her skirt swirled.

Larry grinned at her happiness and clapped his hands. "Wonderful! You're a wonderful dancer."

The Filigree Cross

Fiona turned and dipped one last time, finally collapsing on her bed in laughter.

"I've never seen her do anything like that before," Sue said quietly. "You seem to have an effect on her. I think she's showing off."

"Maybe it's just because I'm a man," Larry offered, getting to his feet.

"No. She's very quiet with Grandpa and the interns."

Fiona sat up and stared at them from her bed. Now she seemed hesitant.

"Do you like dancing? We could bring you some special music," Sue suggested.

"I like my hair better in braids," Fiona said, and began twisting strands between her fingers.

"Well, let me do it." Sue found a wide-toothed comb in the drawer and sat on the edge of the bed. As the comb slid through the russet hair, Larry remembered the feel of it flying across his face. Mother and daughter could have been a painting in the book. The sun streamed in, outlining their bodies in warmth as they bent over a box of ribbons, unable to settle on the right color. Finally Fiona insisted on three, and the thick braid hung down her back, held by gold, crimson, and violet.

AS SOON AS THE DOOR CLOSED behind them Sue turned to Larry. "I've never seen her act so carefree. She must have been so lively, so bright. I wish desperately I could have known her like that." Tears rose in Sue's eyes and she dug in her bag for a tissue.

Dr. Freidman rounded a corner. Immediately, he took Sue's elbow. A tall man, he leaned over her. "Don't be upset. She's very happy right now." Then he included Larry. "Which of you will be overseeing Fiona's care now?"

"Pardon me?" Larry said.

"I always consulted Gillian about Fiona's program. As you know we alternate between periods of intense psychotherapy and rest times, such as she is enjoying now. Personally, I am more than ready to begin counseling again."

Larry looked to Sue for enlightenment, but she shrugged as if she had nothing to offer. "Had Gillian agreed to that?" Larry asked Dr. Freidman.

The doctor bunched his lips together as though sorting his words. "Come into my office."

They settled in chairs and the doctor continued. "You see how content Fiona is now. Gillian hated to interrupt these periods. When we delve into therapy Fiona is forced to return to the pain of her attack. It sends her into depression. She becomes filled with self-loathing. You know about the two suicide attempts years ago. She may be beyond that, but the last time she tried to mutilate herself." He looked back and forth between Larry and Sue. "Did Gillian not tell you?"

Larry sat, riveted. Sue said, "No."

"When Gillian could no longer stand to see her daughter suffer, she would insist we discontinue treatment. Within a few weeks Fiona would seem content again.

"Gillian and I were often at odds. One has to break the barrier down completely for healing. She would

The Filigree Cross

never let me go quite far enough. I think we've wasted time; we need to press ahead."

"What did Fiona do to herself?" Larry asked.

"She slashed at her arms with the end of a paint brush and gouged her thighs."

"Oh, God," Larry murmured, looking at the floor. "No wonder Gillian would back off." He engaged the doctor's eyes. "Today Fiona is happy. That is hard to destroy."

Dr. Freidman leaned forward and spoke softly to them both. "She is a happy *child*. Is that what you want for her? Do you think that is what Fiona would want, were she able to make the decision for herself?"

Larry stood. He was certainly not ready to abandon the cheerful woman he had just visited. "We'll need some time to consider what you've said. I respect your professional opinion and we will give it a good deal of weight."

Dr. Freidman stuck out his hand. "That's all I ask."

"I'll be here at least once a week," Larry added as they moved back out into the hall. "Will Fiona come to trust me?"

"I'm not sure she ever fully accepted Gillian. Anger may not have allowed her to do so. Her attack happened the very first day she stepped out of her parents' care into the world. She had been so safe with them. From what Gillian has told me Fiona was probably over-protected, and as soon as she left that haven she was brutalized, terrorized. Perhaps she still blames Patrick and Gillian for letting her go. If that is part of her thinking, then she might accept you more easily." He paused. "It is very likely that she understands more than she lets on. It will be interesting to see how she does react to you."

At the end of the corridor, wide glass doors opened to a vast expanse of lawn and flowers. Larry motioned toward the doors. "What about taking her outside? Did Gillian take her out?"

"Occasionally, but Fiona feels very insecure beyond these walls. She would rarely go off the grounds. I would like to see her explore the outside. If you can convince her, by all means do it."

Larry shook Dr. Freidman's hand. "I'll make every attempt," he said. "I'll see you next week."

AN HOUR LATER LARRY AND SUE sat in the third row of their theater to watch the rehearsal. The Church of God's Love broadcast twice a week—Wednesday nights and Sundays. Both shows were taped on the preceding Friday. The thirty-row theater had been built just for the tapings, clever camera work making it seem larger to the television audience.

Larry was still shaken from his vision of Fiona attacking her own body. "Gillian didn't let you know what she was dealing with?" he asked Sue.

"My guess is she didn't want anyone's input. Perhaps she didn't want Dr. Freidman to have an ally."

"What a burden."

"Well, *we* have to deal with it," Sue said. "I don't want to just give up on Mother. You've told me how she enjoyed life; surely, as Dr. Freidman said, she would want to get well."

"At whatever cost?"

"I think so."

The Filigree Cross

They sat silent for a few moments then part of the choir filed onstage, followed by Sue's assistant and their celebrity guest. The woman had been a Broadway sensation thirty years before. She professed to be a true Christian, and her singing voice was still strong. Mark's press releases told of how God had come into her life when she was at the height of her commercial success, when the trappings of fame had almost defeated her soul.

Unfortunately, she now suffered with osteoporosis. Her hunched stance made her seem even shorter than her five feet, three inches. The assistant producer moved her from place to place on the stage. She all but disappeared when standing in front of the choir, and when they tried a raised platform behind the lectern, she looked like a puppet. But she needed somewhere to rest her notes.

Sue approached the apron of the stage and made some suggestions which Larry couldn't hear. Apparently they decided to use a decorative music stand and put her at the side of the stage, in front of the six-foot-long flower bed. For the broadcast it would be filled with fresh-cut blossoms.

When she returned to her seat Sue explained. "I'll keep the flower level low," she said. "And I've suggested she wear a straight full-length, pale blue gown. That will add a little stature."

Still unsure, Larry said, "Tell Billy to pull in for a lot of closeups."

"If you were a famous but aging beauty, would you be happy with a lot of closeups?" Sue asked. "Relax, it'll be okay. Luckily Jimmy's not too tall."

Just then the Hawaiian singer entered from the wings, his bronze coloring set off by a brilliant flowered shirt and white pants. Larry noticed Sue sit back in her chair and cross her legs. She unconsciously ran one hand up and down her thigh as she watched Jimmy.

The music director keyed the six-piece combo. The choir did the introduction, then the duet began. The woman was hesitant at first but Jimmy encouraged her, looking directly into her eyes. She smiled and relaxed. Jimmy's fine tenor rose, perfectly underlined by her more mature voice.

Larry nodded, now happier, and turned to Sue. She was smiling, her eyes locked on the Hawaiian.

He leaned over and whispered, "Are you and Jimmy an item? Why have I been kept in the dark?"

"No one's kept you in the dark," she whispered back. "You sometimes don't pay attention."

They watched the rehearsal wind down and Sue waved, dismissing the last people from the stage. "Fine work," she said. "Thank you."

She and Larry remained seated, Sue making notes on a clipboard.

"Back to you and Jimmy," Larry said. "Are his intentions honorable? He's not chasing the boss's granddaughter is he?"

Sue snapped around to face him. "That's none of your business. I can't believe you said that. And why wouldn't he chase me, boss's granddaughter or not?" Her eyes blazed.

"Oh, damn, I'm sorry. I didn't mean it like that. You know I feel like you're my own daughter. I'm just being protective, like a father would be."

The Filigree Cross

"Well, I don't need your help." She began to stand.

Larry touched her arm, motioning her back into her seat. "Don't be angry. Please. I truly didn't mean anything. If you like Jimmy I'm sure he must be a first-rate guy."

Sue relaxed back into her chair and her face softened. "He is. But let me turn the tables on you. Your own love life seems to have slowed to a crawl again. Or am I missing something? What happened to Sandra? I liked her a lot, and we haven't seen her for a month or more. What happened?"

"The usual."

Sue sighed, exasperated. "Sandra is beautiful, and bright, and she adores you—"

"I really thought she might be the one. But I just couldn't promise her what she needed."

Sue laid her hand on his arm. "Larry, not again."

"I know. I'm absolutely hopeless."

Sue twisted in her seat and took his hands in her own.

"Larry, I think this goes beyond your love for Mother. You seem to try to make it difficult for people to get close to you. Give someone a chance. Give yourself over to it. Mother would hate it if she knew she was keeping you from loving someone else. She would want you to be completely happy."

Sue released his hands and straightened. "Did you ever think that it's easy for you to love her for that very reason, because she can't love you back?"

Larry slumped in his seat. He felt his face deflate, his cheeks draw down. No, that wasn't the case with Fiona. He loved her for her spirit and her soul; his feelings had nothing to do with the impossibility of the situation. But Sue's words came too close to what he'd been struggling with since Gillian's death and the subsequent letter. Was he more comfortable being unloved by God? Any love carried a price, but *His* love—it would surely devour a person whole.

Sue leaned close and kissed him on the cheek. "I had better go say goodbye to our guest if I haven't missed her already."

Larry stayed in his seat. Gillian's word—charlatan—had burned itself into his consciousness, where it festered. The fear that he really was a sham, despite the love of his devoted followers, haunted him. If true, how could he change himself? In order to gain God's love and to preach His message properly, would he have to become another Patrick, fingering Bible pages by the hour? The picture frightened him. To give himself over so completely—no, that was not something he could ever do.

The Filigree Cross

CHAPTER ELEVEN

"HOW WAS FIONA?" PATRICK ASKED.

Larry saw he was tired, slouched in his favorite green chair in robe and slippers. Patrick seemed to ask the question by rote, not really wanting to hear that, of course, she was just the same.

Larry smiled, sipping at his coffee. "Actually, she was quite charming. She danced for us."

Patrick's jaw dropped. "Danced? What do you mean?"

"She mimicked some ballerinas in a Degas painting. It was delightful."

A spot of color appeared on each of Patrick's cheeks as he absorbed the image. "Well, I'd sure like to have seen that. Every time I've been to visit, and I know that's not nearly often enough, she's been so quiet I just want to shake her and say, 'come to your senses.' Isn't that stupid? I know I'm an egotistical fool, but I just hate it that she doesn't know me, or won't admit it. And as highly-touted as that hospital is, it gives me the creeps."

"Well, when she gets more used to me, I'm going to bring her home for visits. Maybe that will be easier for you."

The old man's face brightened. "Oh, would you? I'd love that, to have her sit here with me." His head wobbled a bit as he controlled his emotions.

"Today's rehearsal went slowly, but we've got it pretty much nailed down now." He hitched forward in his chair and put his coffee cup on the side table. "Patrick, will you please do a short service at the second taping? We could use your help. Especially since Gillian's passing. I think people want to see that you're carrying on, that you're back with us."

Patrick hesitated.

"If you're not up to it—"

"Well, I could say a few words, for Gillian. She'd like that."

STANDING IN THE WINGS, Patrick fidgeted, seemed unsteady on his feet. I hope I've not brought him back too soon, Larry thought. He pressed Patrick's arm. "Ready?"

"I just realized, this is the first time I've addressed a congregation without Gillie at my side. She made me feel up to every task."

"You don't have to do it today. I'll go on out if you like."

"No. Some day it must be faced."

The music died, indicating his cue, and still Patrick stood, uncertain.

"What would Gillian say to you if she were here?" Larry asked.

The Filigree Cross

"I can hear her. 'Give them something to hold on to.'" He took a deep breath. "I'm okay now, son."

Larry took his arm. As they moved to the center of the stage Patrick received a great reception. The small studio audience sounded many times its size as they stood and applauded, some even shouting his name. Patrick raised his hand in response, and the applause increased still more.

"Thank you all so much." Patrick struggled to be heard over the crowd. He lowered his head to pray. Everyone sat down and silence descended.

"Dear, precious Lord." He spoke slowly, deliberately, trying to overcome his slur. Larry realized how much he'd missed hearing that voice, the one that spoke so clearly what was in the man's heart.

"We've come today to be blessed, dear Lord, to be touched. We close our eyes, unclench our fists and bow our heads to You, leaving ourselves vulnerable. That's our trust in You. We carry no defenses into Your presence. Let us feel the brush of Your breath on our necks as we bend to Your will. We know You understand our weaknesses and will help if we but ask. We ask You now, dear God. Keep us from petty fears, for they block out understanding. Melt our anger, for it shuts out love. Deliver us from our selfishness, which can only lead to solitude. Thus we pray in Jesus' name, Amen."

Patrick cleared his throat as the audience breathed deeply and shifted in their seats, then continued in a conversational tone. "I've seldom envied the Lord," he said. Encouraging murmurs and low chuckles reverberated in the audience. Larry could feel the cameraman zooming in.

"The Lord has much to do; I've never wished for His job. But I have to admit that I'm jealous of Him today. He has our Gillian."

Patrick hesitated, biting at his lip. Larry crossed his fingers.

"She'll serve Him more directly now. And if she does half the job she did here on earth serving all of us, well . . ." He let his smile say the rest.

"It's wonderful to be back here with you tonight. I think I'll stay." He turned to Larry. "Larry, could you get me a chair?"

Larry hurried backstage and brought a folding chair. Patrick had moved nearer the choir. "Just here," he said. Larry deposited the chair, and Patrick sank into it.

The script called for Larry to speak next. But he sensed the audience was not in the mood for his rousing presentation just now. They were introspective, quietly open. He suspected the millions on the other side of the camera were, too.

He motioned to the choir director. "Let's do 'The Old Rugged Cross' for Gillian."

Responding to a raised hand, the choir rose as one, bursting into song, as prepared as if they had anticipated this change in the program. Larry remembered that Gillian had liked this hymn, in spite of the disclaimer of her faith. 'I'll cling to the old rugged cross, and exchange it one day for a crown.' Larry wanted to think that she hadn't totally given up hope of finding God, that maybe she had clung precariously, hoping for enlightenment. He bent his head and asked Patrick's God to bring her in.

The Filigree Cross

A wash of loneliness flooded through him. Was there a God who could bring *him* in?

MARK McLAREN SCOWLED as he watched from the wings. He ran his left hand down the back of his head a couple of times, smoothing his perfect haircut. His eyes were on Patrick, who was leaning back in his chair. The old man looked worn out. When Patrick died, what would happen to the church? Everything would hinge on Larry. He supposed Larry could come up with some kind of degree or credential that would pass muster but probably most of his followers wouldn't even care should they find out he was not ordained. They had bestowed divinity upon him.

Mark envied Larry, but he had to admire the man's sense of propriety. While intoning the Lord's name in the most enthusiastic manner or exhorting the congregation to climactic devotion, he never quoted scripture or suggested that his way was the one to follow. Mark smirked. Probably Larry didn't know any scripture.

Sue came up from behind, interrupting his thoughts.

"A good service, don't you think?" she asked quietly.

"Yeah, it's going really well. But I was just looking at Patrick. Is he okay? He looks beat."

"Grandpa's doing fine. I think tonight has been good for him. It will be the best thing for him to get back to preaching. I'm going to ask him if he's up to going on the next road trip."

"Really?" Mark asked. "Do you think that's wise?"

Marlene Baird

"Only three cities, one service in each. Eight days. I think he'll be fine."

"Well, it would be great for the ratings."

Sue punched him playfully on the shoulder as she moved away. "Do you ever think of anything else?"

"That's what you pay me for, isn't it?"

CHAPTER TWELVE

JOHNNY CAMERON KNEW his grandmother was waiting impatiently in her room; she'd been ready for two hours. She had insisted on getting dressed when the home health care nurse was there because her new outfit, a two-piece navy dress trimmed in white, required a lot of buttoning and fussing with before it sat just right. It would be another hour before they could decently leave the house, though he suspected she would gladly set out immediately and sit in an empty auditorium for that hour.

"Johnny," she said, as she appeared in the doorway to his bedroom. "Do you think they have huge buses like the rock stars?"

"Who?"

"Well, the Church of God's Love people, of course. There's such a lot of them. Reverend Brannigan and Larry Broadfellow, sometimes a famous guest speaker, that huge choir and the musicians. Must be forty or fifty men and women there. Then there's Jimmy Makaani and his six back-up singers. And think of all the off-stage help they must need to get such a show into production."

Marlene Baird

"I'd guess that most of them fly and the workers drive trucks full of gear and stuff. I can't imagine that old minister in a bus."

"You mean Reverend Brannigan," she admonished, but she was in far too good a mood to make much of it. She looked at her watch. "What do you think they're doing now?"

Johnny slumped against his bureau. "Maybe eating. Maybe wondering what there is to see in Minneapolis. I don't know."

"What are you going to wear?"

He stood straight and opened his arms wide. "What you see is what you get." He had on clean jeans, a T-shirt, and a bulky jacket.

"Oh, dear. Why not your nice dress jacket?"

"Gram, that hasn't fit me for two years. The sleeves come up to my elbows."

"We should have bought you one."

"No one is going to care. You've seen those audiences on TV; some people get all duded up and some people don't. It doesn't matter. But you look nice."

She smiled shyly. "Thank you." She checked her watch. "How soon can we go?"

"Do you want to leave now?"

"Well, I'll bet the parking will be awful."

"I'll get the van," he said, touching her arm as he passed her, "and your coat."

"Oh, just a sweater," she said, adjusting her collar. "I won't be outside that long."

The Filigree Cross

IN THE VAN, AS THEY spun down the highway, Gram began to hum. Johnny envied her her happiness, but was confused by it.

"Gram, can I ask you a personal question?"

"Certainly."

"This thing about the church, I mean—" He called up his courage. "Well, I don't understand why you send them money. What can they do for you? What have they ever done for you?"

"Oh, Johnny, I don't send them money so they'll do something for me. I send them money because I'm so grateful, and I think God is responsible for my great blessing."

"What great blessing, Gram? You can't walk without terrible pain. You can barely see the TV anymore. Your husband left you high and dry, and your daughter"—he never referred to her as his mother—"is a wasted druggie. So, what great blessing, Gram?"

She reached across the seat and patted his thigh. "Why you, of course," she said, and went back to her humming.

Johnny saw maybe fifty cars huddled close to the main entrance to the stadium but otherwise the vast parking lot was empty.

"Oh, dear, we really are early," Gram said.

Johnny pulled the van to the curb, brought her chair around, and helped his grandmother into it. Though it took him only a couple of minutes to park the van, by the time he got back to her a uniformed attendant had rushed from inside.

"Welcome," he said, stationing himself behind her.

"Oh, I don't need a push," she said, proudly handling the wheelchair.

Once they were inside, Stan, as his name tag labeled him, asked for their tickets. "Best seats in the house," he said, smiling.

With Stan leading, they wound through cement tunnels, Johnny's eyes on the lookout for passages to team dressing rooms. As they emerged onto the playing field he stared upward at the ceiling of the massive dome, its arching pattern lost in the white glare of piercing spotlights.

The stadium echoed, cavernous and hollow with so few people in their seats. A huge stage had been erected where the pitcher's mound would be, with runways that stretched toward first and third bases. Giant speakers banked either side. The set-up reminded Johnny more of a rock concert than a church service. He estimated that over half of the fifty thousand seats were in a position to see the stage.

On the field between the pitcher's and the catcher's positions, an area had been overlaid with plywood that held maybe two hundred chairs, and in the center was an open space for wheelchairs.

As soon as they got situated in the first row, another uniformed person said, "Welcome," and handed them a folded flyer. The caption read, "Our Beginning—Terre Haute, IN." A picture of a very simple wooden meeting hall graced the front flap. Inside, the program introduced the people who would be on stage and quoted a few verses of scripture.

Maureen maneuvered her wheelchair to be close to him, and Johnny settled low in his seat. These chairs were a lot more comfortable than the stadium seats. He

The Filigree Cross

hadn't been able to get to many Twins games, and when he did come he sat in the stratosphere. Bad luck, his first decent seat and he was going to be looking at pitchers with a different delivery.

"Look at the wonderful flowers on the stage," Gram whispered.

"You don't have to whisper, Gram."

Dazzled, she cooed over the display. Johnny recognized roses the size of softballs, chrysanthemums, and lilies, but a dozen other varieties also burst from huge pots and spilled over the edges of planters. Johnny could smell their aroma. A heavy dark blue drape, maybe velvet, about thirty feet high, stretched wing-like back from either side of the platform, creating a private backstage area.

Johnny squinted upward, trying to see how they suspended that much heavy material, but the details were lost against the floodlights. Someone was testing the spotlights; they criss-crossed the dusty air and three levels of red-carpeted stage. Off to the right, clustered around a glistening ebony grand piano, sat an electric keyboard, two electric guitars, a set of drums, and several instrument cases that looked as if they contained violins.

Slowly, an air of expectancy grew inside the dome and the air began to hum as people filed into their seats and muttered or prayed among themselves. He checked his watch. Everyone, it seemed, was a little early. He hoped that the evening would live up to Gram's expectations. If Larry Broadfellow would only come down those few steps and shake her hand. He glanced at the heavy draperies again. Maybe he could make it happen.

"Gram, I need to go to the bathroom. I'll be right back."

Once he was out of her sight he wound his way through rows and down aisles until he reached the edge of one of the blue drapes. He pulled the pamphlet from his pocket and wrote his request around the edge. A bulky man in a plain dark suit approached and asked him to please return to his seat.

"I'd be really grateful if you could give this to Mr. Broadfellow." Johnny handed the man the note and left before he could say no.

LARRY SAT IN THE DIM RECESSES of the wings. He had moved through the day like a sleepwalker. Normally, just before a service, he could shake off any mood. But now, minutes before he would have to begin, lethargy dragged at him. He'd self-diagnosed a mild depression and that did not concern him. Not being able to muster enthusiasm for an imminent service, however, was more serious.

Heavy steps drew his attention to an approaching security guard.

"Mr. Broadfellow, a young man asked me to give this to you." He handed Larry the pamphlet and returned to his post.

Larry studied the picture, then rubbed his thumb over the sepia shingles and planked door of the old hall. It had started out so simply. He had stepped in to help Patrick and Gillian when they were distraught, their church threatening to die, and somehow it had all turned around. Now Larry felt in need of help, but who would step in for him? The church had become a living thing and he one of its crucial legs. Extricating himself,

The Filigree Cross

even temporarily, would topple it. All around him the church's lifeblood hummed. He heard cables sliding, cameras shifting, instruments being tuned and, somewhere behind him, the choir quietly finding their notes. This performance was going to happen as sure as night would fall, and Larry could no more neglect his duty than the moon could choose to hide.

He turned the pamphlet to follow the writing scribbled along its edge. This evening was apparently the highlight in the life of a good Christian woman, Maureen Cameron, who had known few pleasures. Would Larry maybe acknowledge her? She would be sitting in the first row, in a wheelchair, in a navy and white dress.

Larry rose, slowed by the weight of responsibility, and walked to the curtain. Drawing it open a few inches, he found Maureen Cameron.

Larry pulled a cell phone from his inside pocket. With the touch of two buttons he was talking to the manager of the lighting crew.

"Eric, look down. First row, an older woman in a wheelchair, with a young man." He saw a couple of spotlights waver over that general area, then heard Eric's voice.

"Yeah. I got her."

"When I raise my right hand, my *right* hand, and begin to address the audience, be ready. Her name's Maureen Cameron."

"Got it." The line went dead.

MAUREEN CLENCHED JOHNNY'S HAND. "Did you feel that? That light pass over us?" Her eyes shone like she'd seen the Resurrection.

"Gram, it wasn't God's light. The spot man must have bumped his elbow on the lamp." Johnny immediately regretted his words. She thought it was a sign. What would have been the harm? He was about to apologize for his remark when they were plunged into darkness. Suddenly the air was filled with a glorious burst of voices. They came from nowhere, and everywhere. Even Johnny could hear the conviction of the singers, perfected by hours of practice. The tune was familiar to him, though he couldn't have named it. Sung in rounds, rich bass voices overlaid altos, tenors, sopranos, all identifiable, but a necessary part of the whole. Johnny felt his grandmother shiver; she withdrew her hand from his to grip her Bible.

Huge gold crosses of light appeared on the dark drapes. Then spotlights picked out breaks in the fabric, and the choir filed in. They wore burgundy gowns with broad white collars, setting off faces that glowed as they sang. They carried no music, except in their hearts. The hair on Johnny's neck bristled.

The stage lights brightened in increments until it was fully lit. As soon as the choir was in place, the pace changed dramatically, and they began a rousing gospel song. Johnny hadn't noticed the musicians come onstage, but suddenly there they were. The pianist, a lovely redhead in a blue sequined dress, pounded out a near-boogie beat. The drummer picked it up, then the electric keyboard and guitars. Some in the congregation could not keep from clapping in rhythm.

A man in a white suit with a wide-collared Hawaiian shirt strode to the front of the stage. He swung his arms wide and clapped his hands together,

The Filigree Cross

encouraging the entire audience to do the same. Then he began a song, exhorting the audience to repeat the words with him.

> *Because He died for me; because He died*
> *for me*
> *I will live for Him.*
> *One day when I was lost*
> *He died upon the cross.*
> *Because He died for me; I will live for Him.*

The same few lines were repeated several times. People joined in, hesitantly at first, then, as the words became familiar, with growing gusto. They stood and swayed and clapped. The effect was so electrifying, so charged, that Johnny pictured the dome lifting right off the ground and spinning them away. The Twins never had it so good, he thought. And for the first time in his life, he realized that worship took many forms.

LARRY STOOD WITH PATRICK behind the curtain.

"Listen to that. What a great crowd," Patrick said. "The Lord has been busy since we were in Minneapolis last."

"Yes," Larry replied. "We could have put the stage in center field and filled the whole place."

"Oh, well, that too," Patrick muttered.

Jimmy Makaani was leaving the stage, opposite where they stood.

"You ready?" Larry asked. Patrick nodded; his sermon would immediately follow Larry's first appearance. Larry clicked his mike to the on position and drew three deep breaths.

As the singers' voices faded and the audience felt for their seats, Larry strode out, his long legs eating up the stage.

"Oh, we're celebrating *tonight*!" he shouted, punching the air. Shouts and clapping rolled among the congregation. He paced the full length of the stage and spoke over the noise. "We're celebrating because the Savior loves us. We don't deserve it; we don't even *ask* for it very often, but there it is. And *here* it is!" His arm swung wide, taking in the entire audience. Another burst of enthusiasm. He coaxed them to more shouts, until he felt the tempo begin to wane. Then he stopped at center stage, hands at his side, waiting.

When silence descended he spoke quietly.

"And I have as much to celebrate as anyone. You've seen that picture on the front of your handouts." A rustle in the audience. "That building—a paint-stripped, roof-leaking, spider's paradise. In that simple place I first spoke to people about God and prayer. It was a time of terrible, terrible pain for Reverend Brannigan's family, a time of soul-searching and wrestling with the Almighty." Larry paused, then raised his eyebrows and whispered into the mike, "He won." A few quiet laughs. Then he continued. "Just a few months before that building became the church's home, I was a drunk. I had no home, and didn't care for one. I had no friends, needed no one. I had no hope, wanted that less than anything. Hope meant dreams, and dreams meant disappointment. I literally stumbled into a gospel meeting Reverend Brannigan was

The Filigree Cross

conducting in a tent raised in a farmer's field. He and Gillian and their lovely daughter saved my life."

Larry moved around the stage, as if strolling and thinking. Talking about the early days was helping his mood. "I always give credit for my salvation to Patrick and his family. But Patrick gives all the credit to God, and Patrick knows a lot more about this kind of thing than I do. Did God send me down that very road at that very moment, when I could have been a thousand other places? Did God make them open their hearts to a wastrel? Did God make me weak enough to stay and strong enough to last? Does God give me the words, day after day, night after night?"

He could feel the audience pressing the answer upon him. Larry shouted, "Yes! Yes! And He has the patience to see it through to the end."

Please, let it be true, he thought.

He looked into the eyes of those in the front rows, ranging from left to right and back again. "Many of you probably thought I had come to full realization some time ago, that the reason I'm on this stage is because I know the Lord personally. No. I'm on this stage because I know God *exists*. I know that His message is being lived because there are so many Patricks and Gillians out among you."

He poked at his chest. "No, *I'm* not a good example of God's handiwork." He passed the microphone from his right hand to his left and pointed to the seats, sweeping back and forth, now with his right hand. "You are the true fruits of God's labor. People like you, Maureen Cameron, right down here, visiting for the first time under our new tent."

Marlene Baird

AS THE SPOTLIGHT SWUNG over her wheelchair, Maureen, overcome by being addressed directly and lost in awe at Broadfellow's attention, unconsciously rose from her chair and took a hesitant step toward the stage.

Johnny jumped up and grabbed her. "Gram!" He took her arm and pulled her back into her chair. A shock ran through the audience.

Immediately Larry Broadfellow was beside her. "No. Let me come to you." He kneeled at her side.

"Why did you come here tonight, Maureen?"

Maureen Cameron's hand went to her chest and she took a moment to get her breathing under control.

"Well, you remember, you invited us."

Larry's mind raced. Invited them? No one told him anything about that.

"Of course," he said smoothly, "but what else do you want to have happen here tonight?"

"I want to thank the Lord for my wonderful grandson, Johnny." She patted Johnny's arm and the spotlight expanded to include him. "He cares for me all the time, sacrifices a lot. But you know that. I wrote you about it."

Larry lost his animation. The audience would now think this was a set-up; the moment had lost all spontaneity.

"Yes. You wrote us about him. And I'm so glad that you both came tonight so we can witness such faith and such love." Larry faltered, searching for words. He felt he'd been pulled into some sort of trap—but how had it happened?

"I'd like some prayers said for Johnny," the woman said, "like I asked in my letter."

The Filigree Cross

Johnny sank deeper into his chair, his face flushing red.

Larry glanced at the young man. Hoping it might be safer to talk to the boy, he said, "Johnny, will you stand with me?" He reached across Maureen to take Johnny's arm, urging him to his feet. The young man's body was tense; he was obviously uncomfortable, and Larry thought maybe he'd compounded his problem.

He turned Johnny to face the audience. "If, tonight, right now, we were all to offer a prayer on your behalf, what would you ask of God?"

Johnny, blinded by the spotlight, squinted at Larry. "That Gram have no more pain in her back and legs."

A collective sigh rose from the crowd.

Larry hugged the young man and whispered, "God bless you," and climbed back to the stage.

He stood still until the quiet became awkward. He should probably say some kind of prayer for Johnny, as Maureen had asked, but the situation seemed contrived, and the words weren't there. This entire scenario was filling him with insecurity. He dug deep; he desperately needed a way off the stage. He turned his back to the crowd, unbuttoned his jacket, and loosened his tie.

Suddenly he spun and jolted them with shouts, repeatedly jamming a finger toward the upper decks. "Can you possibly think that the Lord doesn't live in these two hearts? No! He is *within* these people. He is within all of you, and I am grateful beyond expression to be even a small part of it."

Larry dropped the mike to the carpet and rushed from the stage, his jacket flying out behind him.

Marlene Baird

HOLY SHIT, MARK McLAREN THOUGHT, in his perch in the second tier of seats. Thousands of people were holding their breaths. He shook his head in wonder as the choir began a soothing hymn. He had to admit it; Larry was a genius, nothing less. Where the hell did he come up with the words? Where did he learn to read people so well? That young boy saying he wanted only for his grandmother to be well . . . what if the kid had been tongue-tied with nerves? Or asked for a new car? Larry would have overcome that, too.

Patrick walked out to take the stage, Bible in hand, the choir fading behind him. Patrick held the Bible open before him but had no need to read as he recited some scripture. Mark let his mind run back over what Larry had said earlier about the tent meetings. The mystique of the Brannigans' beginnings was something they sometimes teased audiences with, but this was the first time Larry had used it to tell his own story. One line replayed in Mark's head. Larry had said something about Patrick and Gillian and their lovely daughter having saved him. Where was the lovely daughter? Mark had never met her, never heard a word about her. Was Larry referring to Sue's mother? Had she, perhaps, died? Even if that were the case, he couldn't imagine her name not having been mentioned at some point.

CHAPTER THIRTEEN

LARRY FUMED IN FRUSTRATION, pacing the dressing room. He jerked off his jacket and threw it on the chair. Patrick would be on now, then Jimmy—he had a few minutes to settle himself down.

He tried to remember the audience reaction at the end of his speech, but could not. He'd been too into himself. He hoped his suddenly leaving the stage had seemed somewhat appropriate, that no one guessed he was escaping his own embarrassment. In speaking with that woman he'd answered what he thought to be an innocent request, but, in fact, she almost seemed to expect his attentions. It didn't surprise him that someone had missed her letter, there were so many thousands of entreaties every day. But if her requests had been ignored, how did she end up in the special seating section? Tech's secretary, Theresa, was in charge of VIP seating. As soon as the service was finished he would get her on the phone.

Larry dashed some water on his face, combed his hair, and returned to backstage. Patrick was just finishing his sermon. He led the congregation in a last prayer. He usually simply left the stage when he was finished, but tonight he gave Jimmy Makaani a great introduction, beckoning him to step forward and putting his arm around the younger man's shoulders.

"You all know Jimmy Makaani," Patrick said. An appreciative murmur rumbled through the crowd. "I can stand here and talk to you about God's love. But Jimmy can sing about it, in that God-given voice, and the message becomes more joyous."

Jimmy seemed taken aback at the unexpected compliments and smiled shyly. He rubbed a hand over his head.

"Jimmy started worshiping at an early age, at outdoor services on the Big Island of Hawaii. Can you imagine a lovelier setting in which to learn about the blessings of our Lord? Jimmy's father worked as a cook on a ranch, and his mother was a school teacher. They loved our Savior and brought their son up in a caring, Christian home. And I thank them for that every time I hear his voice raised in praise."

Patrick gave Jimmy a hug and continued. "So I'll get out of the way now and let you enjoy this wonderful expression of our love of God."

As the musicians began the introduction to a set of hymns and gospel songs, Patrick joined Larry backstage, his eyes gleaming.

"He's a fine young man," he said. "Sue's in love with him, you know."

"I suspected," Larry said. He paused, not wishing to break Patrick's fine mood, but he felt the need to apologize for his earlier behavior before he went onstage again. "I'm sorry, about before."

Patrick began to walk away, but Larry took his arm. "Patrick, I'm sorry."

The Filigree Cross

Patrick looked at him, confused.

"The way I left the stage so quickly. It must have put you on the spot."

"Oh, that. Son, don't worry. It was fine. Sometimes the Lord takes hold when we least expect it. He told you to get out of the people's way when they had something to think about, that's all. Did you notice how quiet the auditorium was?"

Larry shook his head. "No. I was too busy running away. Talking with that woman tripped me up, and I couldn't get back into synch. I don't know what came over me."

"You okay now?" Patrick spotted Sue and waved to her. "I need a word with my granddaughter. Doesn't she look wonderful lately?"

Larry's heartbeat returned to normal. If Patrick thought everything was all right maybe the audience did, too. This was what "coming out smelling like a rose" really meant. Once again he shook his head at his good fortune. He was constantly amazed at his own glibness on stage; that what spontaneously came out of his mouth somehow turned out to be right. If God had given him this ability, then why couldn't Larry feel His presence? Why was his soul hollow; the words echoing around inside him reaching others, but not touching his own heart?

Still unsure of his reception, Larry decided to take Patrick back out on stage with him during his last session. He interrupted Patrick's conversation with Sue.

"Will you close it out with me?" he asked.

Patrick grinned, pleased. "Of course, son."

When they walked on stage, Larry raised their joined fists in the air. "Here is a man of God. The rock on which this wonderful church is built. I'm honored to take his hand and bind myself to his loving goodness. Will you join me by taking the hand of the person next to you? Feel our Savior's love flowing between you, up and down the rows, encompassing us all."

Larry stopped speaking as audience members were slow to follow his lead. He allowed the silence to work for him, forcing the congregation to comply before he continued. Then he turned his body toward Patrick, inviting him to speak. Larry needed to hear the voice of a man unencumbered by doubt.

Patrick dropped his head to pray. "Jesus, You are Lord of my life. Let your Spirit come, bearing God's love."

JOHNNY CAMERON, REFUSING TO BOW his head in prayer, stared directly into Larry Broadfellow's face, trying to read it. But as much as he wanted to, he couldn't look at the man with callousness. He didn't want to admit it, but something was happening inside this dome. Sometimes the hush of the crowd was so heavy he felt as though he couldn't breath; another time his chest would expand as if he were being force-fed fresh air. Something tugged at his insides; he felt sad and hopeful at the same time.

He closed his eyes and listened to Reverend Brannigan's prayer. It was about God's embrace of lost souls. Johnny first thought of his mother, but then he realized that he, himself, was being described perfectly. The old man's voice cut through to

The Filigree Cross

something sharp—the hope of a little boy kneeling at his bedside and begging for his grandmother to come and get him. Johnny listened to every point the reverend made. His entire body slumped and he fell so deeply under the spell of the words that, when they ended, he felt he'd been abandoned.

CHAPTER FOURTEEN

DAYS LATER REVEREND BRANNIGAN'S words still rang in Johnny's head. When he recited them, a warmth replaced a hollow inside—a hollow so long familiar that he hadn't realized it could be filled. When he took a deep breath it seemed to spread throughout his entire body instead of just pumping his lungs. The top of his head felt heavier, as if larger thoughts were forming, and he often drifted from the moment to try to grasp them.

"Johnny, what is it?" Gram asked one morning as he sipped at a cup of coffee gone cold.

Johnny blinked. "Gram, I can't stop thinking about that service."

Maureen smiled. "You used to call them shows. Wasn't it wonderful, I mean, to talk right to him?"

Johnny nodded. "I don't know how to say it. I felt something that night." He shrugged and shook his upper body. "It's kind of weird. But it won't go away."

"Do you think it's possible, Johnny," she whispered, "that God touched you?" Her voice was raw with hope.

The Filigree Cross

"I don't know. I never thought it could happen that way. I thought you had to study for years and know the Bible like you do."

"Would you like to read my Bible?"

"Maybe. But Gram, what I'm really thinking about is—"

"Yes?" she urged him. "Say it."

"Could you ever manage without me? Once you said you never would be able to."

Maureen felt tears stinging her eyes. It took considerable effort to control her voice. "Well, what I meant, dear, was that I could never manage without your love and caring. That is different than needing you here with me every day. What are you trying to say?"

Johnny blushed right up to his hairline and tried to chuckle. "It's silly, Gram. Like a kid running away to join the circus. But I want to go to work for Larry Broadfellow. I want to be a part of what happens on that stage and in the audience. I need to know how it works." His voice became animated. "Maybe there's something I could do, like setting up the stage."

Maureen settled back into her chair, loving eyes resting on her grandson. Her mind reached for words that would set him free without guilt. "Nothing would make me happier, Johnny. You know, you've got me spoiled, waiting on me hand and foot. There's a lot of things I could do for myself if I had to. And I could get more help from the home health services. I'd be fine."

She saw the lines in his face ease. Maureen was sure God had a hand in this, but so had Larry Broadfellow. When the evangelist put his arm around

Johnny's shoulders, it had occurred to Maureen that no grown man had ever embraced her wonderful grandson.

"How should I start, Gram?"

"We'll write a letter directly to Reverend Brannigan. I have a feeling that man couldn't disappoint anyone."

Maureen choked back tears. Why was it never easy when God took hold of one's life?

CHAPTER FIFTEEN

ONCE THEY WERE HOME from the tour, Larry made a point of stopping to see Patrick a couple of times a day to make sure he was getting his rest. The travel had been more of an effort than the man wanted to admit. He found Patrick at his desk surrounded by mail. "Why don't you let someone else take care of that?" Larry asked.

"I like to read some of the letters. I wish I had the energy to answer more often."

Patrick held up an envelope. "That young man, Johnny Cameron, is arriving on Thursday. Have we found him a place to live?"

Larry sat in the stuffed chair opposite Patrick's desk. Why did these people keep coming into his life? He'd always known that getting personally involved with someone in the audience was chancy. He regretted more than ever his singling out Mrs. Cameron and her grandson. "The kid from the Minneapolis service who wrote about a job. Sue mentioned it. Apparently one of the cameramen, Billy Sills, has room. He and his wife can put him up for a while. She's expecting a baby in a few months, but that should give this young man time to get on his feet."

"What's the wage? This letter was written by his grandmother. It sounds like she depends on him."

"Patrick, relax. You know we pay everyone well. He'll be fine."

Patrick sat back, satisfied, fingering the envelope.

"Interesting, isn't it?" he asked, with that crooked smile. "His grandmother said he'd never attended church, never read the gospel, never shown any interest in religion whatsoever, until you spoke to them that night."

"Maybe the kid just needs a decent job."

"Stop it, Larry. Why won't you accept God's power working through you?"

Larry shuddered internally. He could never admit to Patrick that his own faith was in shreds and had been for decades. "I guess it's just that I've not been schooled, trained. That makes me feel false sometimes."

"Larry, maybe you did come to preaching through the back door, and you still see yourself as an interloper. But you can't possibly believe that the Lord cares how we come to Him. I think this young man is searching just like you were. Perhaps he is afraid of taking the usual path, perhaps seeing it as a blinding thing that takes away one's personal judgment. So he's making an end run; coming at faith from an unexpected angle. Trying to sneak up on the truth. But God doesn't care what amount of skepticism we bring."

Patrick rose slowly from his chair and came around the desk to put a hand on Larry's shoulder. "And as for

The Filigree Cross

your so-called falseness, so what if we don't do everything just right? Who knows what just right is? The message is bigger than the messenger. Don't ever get confused about that."

Larry patted Patrick's hand and Patrick hobbled slowly to the window.

"You feeling stiffer than usual?"

Patrick turned, rubbing an elbow. "Oh, the doctor says its nothing serious. Some arthritis probably. Gave me some pills, but they upset my stomach. Frankly, I think it's being alone does it."

"Does what?"

"Well, I never felt so achy and ancient when Gillie was around."

Larry wondered how he might help Patrick. "Listen, I'd like to bring Fiona here to the house for a visit. What about this week?"

Patrick's face lit up. "Really? Would she come? That would be wonderful."

TALKING ABOUT JOHNNY CAMERON reminded Larry that he wanted to ask Theresa why Johnny and his grandmother had been in the front row in Minneapolis. He returned to his own house and, reluctantly, called her at the office. Simply talking to Theresa put him on edge; she tried so hard. He told himself he could like her if she were only a bit softer. But he'd known softer women, and few more beautiful. And some, beautiful and soft at the same time. None of them mattered.

"Larry!"

He cringed at the undisguised excitement in her voice.

"What a super surprise. What can I do for you?" The question suggested a multitude of possibilities.

"Theresa, when we were in Minneapolis, there were two people in the front row. A Mrs. Cameron and her grandson."

"Yes?"

"I know you sometimes make those selections."

"Mostly I do. Was that a problem?"

"How did they happen to be there?"

Theresa hesitated, then spoke quickly. "Oh, I remember now. We got a lovely letter from the grandson. Johnny, I think his name is?"

"Yes, Johnny."

"Anyway, he said his grandmother worshipped you and it would mean a lot to them, so we did it. No mystery."

Larry thought she sounded edgy. Had he caught her off guard, or was it just that he hadn't responded to her purring?

He recalled the boy's shyness. "He asked to be put in the front row?"

"No, no." She hesitated again. "Um, he wanted you to say hello to her personally. We knew you don't usually do that, so we did the next best thing."

"We?"

"Oh, I talked it over with Tech."

Larry wondered why on earth Tech would care about these two people.

Theresa interrupted his thoughts. "I heard, though, that, in fact, you did talk to them at the service."

"Yes. The boy sent a note backstage."

"Well that must have pleased her."

"I guess. Thanks, Theresa."

The Filigree Cross

"Is there a problem, Larry?"

"No, not at all. Just curious."

Theresa recovered her seductive voice. "Well, don't be a stranger."

Larry hung up the phone and stood, hands on his hips. Something troubled him about the odd set of circumstances, but he couldn't put his finger on the problem.

A HUGE BANNER, HELD AT EITHER end by bunches of brightly colored balloons, draped the massive entry doors of the mansion. "Welcome Home, Fiona," it read.

"What is that for?" she asked, pointing.

Larry parked the car and took her hand. "It's for you. This is where your father lives. Where you might live one day."

"Is it?"

Larry's spirits fell. He thought she had understood his earlier explanation about visiting Patrick. She'd seemed to pay attention, nodding at appropriate times.

It had taken a lot of persuasion to get her into Larry's car. When Dr. Freidman closed her door she sat bolt upright, her eyes large. The doctor whispered to Larry, "Be careful. Come back as soon as she asks." The doctor had also pressed Larry for a decision on further therapy. Larry answered that he wanted some time to allow Fiona and Patrick to connect; that since Gillian's death Patrick needed this extra comfort. Dr. Freidman had not hidden his disappointment.

Patrick met them at the door. "Fiona, my little girl," he murmured, hugging her to his chest, then planting a kiss on her forehead. Larry hadn't seen so much animation in Patrick in a long time, which reinforced his decisions both bring her and to delay treatment.

Fiona stood back, studying Patrick's face. With her finger she traced the awkward side of his smile, where muscles pulled at the skin. "Does it hurt?" she asked.

"I think you just made it better," Patrick said, and Larry saw his eyes tear.

Patrick took her hand and led her away, as if to claim her for his own. Larry tagged along. They roamed from room to room, Patrick unfazed at her disconnected remarks. When she said, "There should be flowers on the door," he simply said he'd have them painted on immediately. In Patrick's study Fiona stared at the portrait of Gillian. Larry hoped she would ask about not seeing Gillian lately, but after a few moments she simply turned away.

As Patrick finished the tour, Sue came home, and the four of them shared sandwiches and tea. Patrick beamed the whole time. Suddenly Fiona stood and left the room, and Larry and Sue both jumped up. Patrick put out his hand. "Let her go. I've instructed Simon and Gloria to watch the entrances. She won't get far."

But Larry felt responsible. He followed her at a discreet distance, ducking around corners feeling foolish, like a little kid playing games. He stopped in the hallway outside the den and heard her lifting pictures and books. Was she reading—maybe wondering? Was there something she recognized? Eager to know, he stretched his neck to see into the room.

She turned. "You're not a very good tracker you know."

The Filigree Cross

She held a framed photo in her hand—her high school graduation picture. "Who is this?" she asked.

Larry knew she had been presented with this photo time and again over the years. She'd never admitted any interest.

"Who do you think?"

"It's supposed to be me." She buffed the glass surface with the sleeve of her sweater.

"And you don't believe that?"

"She looks too smart."

"Too smart for what?"

"Too smart to be in a hospital."

"Would you like to leave the hospital and live here? Would that make you feel more like the girl in the picture?"

"I don't have her eyes. Look how they sparkle."

Larry reached out to touch the photograph. "But see her hair? You have her hair."

Fiona studied the picture, then replaced it on the side table. "She should braid it," she said flatly. "Can we go back?"

CHAPTER SIXTEEN

JOHNNY THOUGHT MR. AND MRS. Sills were terrific people. He loved the room they gave him to sleep in even though the cot, which was his bed, crowded the space. It sat across the busy room from a beautiful baby's crib, dressed in frills and filled with sweet-smelling blankets and quilts. Two dressers, the drawers painted with ivy leaves, overflowed with stuffed animals. Shelves above a changing table held baby oil, powder, soaps, diapers and washcloths folded into tiny squares.

Marilyn Sills pushed aside some boxes in the closet to make room for Johnny's few things. She apologized for the mobile of jungle animals, already suspended from the ceiling.

"We just couldn't wait," she said, smiling. "We could take it down."

Johnny said to leave it, he liked it.

The first night Johnny lay in the cot, staring upward. Pinpricks of light had been inset in the ceiling, like faraway stars, so it was never truly dark. The baby they were expecting was very lucky.

The Filigree Cross

Johnny recalled his own urine-smelling childhood mattress. He had wet the bed until he was four, and his mother seldom noticed. His first happy memory was when his grandmother showed up one day and took him away. At the time she was a complete stranger, but he felt no hesitation in going with her. She smelled so clean and had a soft face. That night he lay in snow-white sheets, tucked under warm blankets. She had taught him that simple prayer, done on his knees. "Now I lay me down to sleep." The meaning had not been clear at that young age, but it had comforted him.

After a few days, his mother arrived and took him back. For months, whispering his prayer so she couldn't hear, he had added a plea for his grandmother to come for him again. Finally, she did, and she told him he was to stay with her forever. Forever, it turned out, had been only fourteen years, and now he was leaving her. He never thought that would happen. But somehow this coming to Chicago, coming to work for the church, just had to be. He knew Gram understood.

In the dim light Johnny watched the mobile. A rhinoceros swung slowly in the breeze from the window, bumping softly into an elephant's hip. He fell asleep envisioning a huge watering hole at sunset, the shadows of gazelles and long-legged birds stretching out over the rippled water.

IN THE MORNING, over cereal and toast, Billy Sills gave him directions to the studio and told him to check in with Sue, Reverend Brannigan's granddaughter.

Sue welcomed him and explained that they were going to tape two services today, as usual. Johnny saw

Marlene Baird

a lot of activity: people moving equipment and furniture as they rearranged the stage, seemingly to make more room in the center.

"We have a guest choir today for the first taping," Sue explained.

Johnny looked around hoping to see Larry Broadfellow.

Sue consulted with several people about placement of flowers and mikes and the color of the backdrop, then returned to him. "What kind of work have you been doing, Johnny?"

"I've worked at the same convenience store for years. Stocked shelves at first. No, before that I cleaned up. Then I stocked shelves. Then I checked out customers, and in the end I was night manager. Locked up the money, closed up."

"But, you're only how old?"

"Eighteen."

"That's a lot of responsibility for someone so young."

He looked at his feet. "Well, they thought I was a little older. I started there when I was fifteen."

"Did you finish high school?"

Sue looked like a kind lady, but he wasn't ready to tell her that Gram had been really sick for a couple of years and he hadn't gotten any studying done at home.

"Barely. School and me, I don't know, just didn't fit."

"Well, we'll try you at a couple of jobs and see what does fit. How does that sound?"

Johnny beamed. "Anything would be fine," he said.

The Filigree Cross

"Since you already know Billy, I'm going to assign you to him. You'll learn how to care for the cameras, how to anticipate when he needs you to move something, any number of little things."

"Billy's great. Thanks a lot."

AT NOON THE STAGE WAS SET, the choir was in place, and the studio doors were opened to admit the audience. At twelve fifteen Sue addressed the crowd. She reminded them that the service would be taped and that the camera would occasionally swing toward them. They grinned when she said they'd be able to see themselves on Wednesday night. She held up both hands until the room was completely silent, then moved off the stage. Johnny heard someone counting down. Four, three, two.

They were plunged into darkness for a split second. Then the stage lights raised, the choir burst into song, and the building was transformed. Johnny felt a tingle run up his legs. He stood still, trying to identify the feelings he was experiencing. Suddenly someone jerked his arm, pulling him farther behind the curtain. He'd been standing within sight of the audience.

"Sorry," he whispered to the man.

The man held his finger to his mouth. "Shh."

Johnny turned his eyes to the backstage area and finally found Larry Broadfellow. The evangelist was pacing, head down, brow furrowed. He slapped one fist into his other hand time and again. Johnny was surprised to see him so agitated; he wouldn't have believed the man ever had a moment's distress. Johnny felt somehow reassured to see him being so human.

Marlene Baird

Johnny stepped further into the dark recesses to watch Broadfellow. At one point the evangelist stopped walking and rubbed his cheeks vigorously. Then he straightened his jacket and shook his shoulders. He seemed distraught, and a million miles away, but the instant the choir ended their hymn, he spun and walked out into the spotlight, arm raised, smiling, like he'd been born to it.

"I was right all along. He's a chameleon," Johnny muttered. The tingle went out of his legs.

LARRY TOOK A DEEP BREATH and cleared his throat. He connected with the appropriate camera, then cleared his throat a second time. That was unacceptable but he knew they would edit it out. His Adam's apple seemed stuck high in his throat. He turned directly to the audience. The first two rows looked eagerly up at him. He smiled and breathed deeply again, but his mind was empty. All that came to him was that he'd forgotten to pick up his laundered shirts and would be out of clean ones tomorrow. The smile on his face began to feel glued on.

Sue stepped to the wings. "Larry, you okay?" she whispered.

He turned to her with a wave, and nodded. Of course he was okay. It was just another taping. How many thousands had he done without a moment's preparation, without a hint of hesitancy?

Just to be doing something, he walked upstage, dragging a stool forward. He sat on it. People in the audience were now clearing their own throats, as if in sympathy.

The Filigree Cross

He began very quietly, and they had to settle down to hear him. His eyes ranged, taking in the entire audience. "You know, I've always wondered when I might run out of words. Today seems to be the day." Chuckles rose from the onlookers. They didn't believe him. Unexpectedly, a chuckle rose in his own throat and burst out. Panic made his breath catch; he was not in control. He plastered on a smile and made eye contact with the red dot on the camera.

"I've come onto this stage, and many others, hundreds and hundreds of times. Never before have I had to grasp for an idea. But today the thoughts are not coming." He swallowed hard. "The only thing I can figure out is that God has stopped being easy on me."

Larry stood and began to pace slowly. He squared his shoulders, then let them drop, trying to relax.

Sue's heart pounded. She searched out Patrick. "What is he doing? This is not going to play well on the screen."

Patrick simply took her hand. "He's not doing anything. God is. Let him be."

Larry tried a conversational tone. "I've had a good ride. God has sent me millions of words, and I've passed them on to you. My guess is that I've used up my welcome. I've taken too many withdrawals from my heavenly account and not put in enough deposits. Our Lord is patient, but He's no fool. At some point we have to stop counting on His blind forgiveness and face up to ourselves. At some point, surely, He says, this guy isn't paying attention, he needs a shake-up. Let's see what he can do on his own for once."

Marlene Baird

He paused, stretching his arms wide, fingers extended. "Well, I'm here to tell you, that I can't do a single thing on my own."

The silence told him that was not what they wanted to hear. They had come to be buoyed by Larry Broadfellow, to ride on his coattails to exultation. His mission was to grease the path.

The quiet was broken by a man in the audience who, mercifully, muttered, "Amen, brother."

Larry pointed in the general direction of the voice, grasping for an opportunity to keep talking. "Did you hear that? Amen, brother. Amen, brother. What do you think that man meant when he said that to me? He meant, we're in this together. Sinking and swimming and taking turns doing it. Passing around the life jackets, hoping there will be enough.

"Well, what if there aren't *enough* life jackets? What if God turns away for a moment and lets us swallow a little salt water? What if He lets it get into our lungs, and we gasp and flail because we've taken Him for granted."

Larry stopped at center stage, leaning forward. "Well, I'll tell you what." He poked at his own chest. "I wish I'd learned to swim better. I wish I hadn't held onto the life preserver so long. I wish I had let go just once. Of course, that takes courage. Your body sinks; the water fills your nose, then makes you blink. That's not comfortable." Larry felt as though he were being sucked under now. He gulped air. "So we grab onto the floater again, pull ourselves up and breathe easy. We get dressed up and go to church on Sunday. Or we tune in, sitting in our easy chairs, and worship from home.

The Filigree Cross

We take care of our own souls the easiest way possible."

It occurred to him that he had just described his own lack of dedication. He didn't work hard on the stage several times a week because it was hard. He did it because it was easy, or had been.

"We are forever asking the Lord for blessings. We ask for, and receive, forgiveness. We ask for, and receive, comfort. We ask for, and receive, life everlasting. Those are a lot of withdrawals."

He knew they hated this lecture; brow-beating they could get any number of places. This was when he should change his tactic, start making them feel good. But he had become one of them—a member of the audience, waiting for enlightenment.

SUE LOOKED OUT AT THE FLAT FACES, hoping the camera was avoiding them. She tried to get Larry's attention, to see if he needed some kind of help. She cringed to think what McLaren would make of it when he saw the tape.

Desperate, she approached Patrick again. "Will you go out and save him? Please, for me?"

"My guess is he's almost finished," Patrick said.

LARRY RETURNED TO THE STOOL. "I've no right to sit here and judge you when I'm so overdrawn. So, I'm going to take a sabbatical."

Larry heard Sue gasp from the wings. The audience, though, didn't seem to have caught his meaning. "I leave you in the best of hands. The very best of hands. Reverend Brannigan is a man who always has excess funds available in his heavenly account. He's the man to show you the way to God."

Larry looked to the wings and motioned to Patrick. Patrick walked on stage, Bible in hand.

"Thank you, son." Patrick said, his voice wavering. "We'll miss you."

The men embraced. Larry clung to Patrick; held on like he had at nine years old in Trinity Church. Tears streamed down his cheeks, wetting Patrick.

"It's okay, son," Patrick whispered. "It's okay."

Larry pulled away, waved to the audience and left the stage.

CHAPTER SEVENTEEN

"I GUESS YOU'VE HEARD SOMETHING about this by now," Sue said, starting the video. She had invited Mark to watch the tape in her office in hopes that she might be able to temper his reaction.

"It can't possibly be as bad as I've been told," he said, shaking an aspirin from a small bottle and swallowing it. She motioned toward a side table where a carafe of cold water and glasses sat. He shook his head, intent on Larry's performance. Within a few minutes his mood escalated from sour to barely-contained anger. By the time Larry walked off the stage, Mark was pacing the room. "Who the hell does he think he is? He's destroying the livelihoods of over a hundred people right here in Chicago, without a moment's notice."

Sue turned off the tape, aware that Mark's real concern would be for himself, not the other ninety-nine.

He circled the space between her desk and the door like a dog with no place to settle, his mouth drawn into a tight scowl.

Marlene Baird

"We don't have to air it," he said, running one hand over his hair. He looked to her for confirmation. "We say he's on vacation, or taking a breather. Anything. But people don't have to hear him say that God's given up on him. What the hell was he thinking?"

Sue turned away from his outburst and walked to the window. She had no answer for that; it was her own question. Immediately after the second taping she had gone home to search out Larry but his car was not in his garage. She had watched from the main house until she saw him drive up, then gone down to his place. When he didn't answer her knock or the doorbell, she opened the door and called to him.

His rough voice answered, "In the den."

She hurried down the hall, fearing he was ill, and saw him refolding a letter. He tucked it into a metal box which he locked, pocketing the key. An unopened whiskey bottle stood on his reading table. Her grandmother had told her that Larry was once a drinker, but she'd never seen liquor in his home before.

"Are you okay?" She searched his face. His eyes were bleary from crying, and dark-circled. His mouth, always ready with a smile for her, dragged down at the corners. Scared, she took his shoulders. "What's happened, Larry? Are you sick?"

Larry removed her hands. "No. Just worn out. I'm sorry about the taping. You don't have to use it."

"That's beside the point. What happened out there on that stage?"

"Just what I said. God left me high and dry."

The Filigree Cross

Sue could see that he was moving rapidly from misery to self-pity. "Larry, get a grip. God doesn't let people down. People let themselves down."

"Okay. I let myself down. What does it matter? I'm useless. If I don't have words, I don't exist."

"That's crazy."

He sat down, and motioned for her to do the same. "No, Sue, it's not crazy. Think about it. I'm Larry Broadfellow, evangelist. I'm not Larry Broadfellow, father. Not a son. Not a husband. Not even a lover. So if words fail me I cease to exist."

Though she wanted to shout at him, Sue kept her voice calm. "Patrick loves you like a son. You're a combination father and brother to me. Gillian loved you. That's more than a lot of people have, to say nothing of the millions in your audience. Stop feeling sorry for yourself."

He paused, and his eyes drifted to the metal box. "Yes, Gillian did love me, even though she knew."

"What did she know?"

Larry took a deep breath, and stood in front of her chair. "Sue, you don't need to listen to this maudlin stuff. It's nothing to do with you. I've dumped a mess in your plate, and I am truly sorry. But there is nothing I can do about it."

"You mean, right at this moment. You *are* going to come back to us."

"I have no idea."

Sue slumped back into her chair. This was unbelievable, ludicrous. Everyone had been worried about her grandfather's health for years and wondered what would happen to the church if he should get really ill again. No one had ever dreamed that Larry would be the one to leave them.

He pulled her up from the chair and led her to the door. As they passed the table she picked up the bottle of whiskey. "Why don't I take this with me?"

He shrugged. "Sure."

MARK WAS IMPATIENT WITH her silence. "Well, what do you think? Patrick can make some explanation for Larry's temporary absence."

She turned back to face him. "I'm not sure it will be temporary," she said.

Mark's face opened up like a child's. "What do you mean, not temporary?"

"He's burned out, Mark. I'm worried about him."

"Well, he sure as hell wasn't worried about any of us when he decided to spill his guts in front of millions of viewers."

"It was only a taping, Mark. Larry knew that."

Mark threw his arms in the air in exasperation. "Only a taping. What the hell do we do now? Show 'The Best of Broadfellow?'" Sue saw him struggle for control, to keep from saying too much. He grabbed the door handle. "I still say we can't air it. See if Patrick agrees."

He shut the door just short of a slam. Sue didn't take it personally. His job was on the line if Larry left them. No one harbored any illusions about Patrick, in his poor state of health, being able to carry the ministry for long without Larry.

THAT NIGHT PATRICK AND SUE sat quietly over dinner. Friday's second taping had not gone well

The Filigree Cross

without Larry. Neither wanted to talk about that. Anyway, Larry's problems were foremost on both their minds.

"Have you talked to him?" Sue asked.

"I offered. He wants to be alone."

"What do you think is going on? Maybe he just needs a break."

Patrick shook his head, swallowing a bite of roast beef. "No. It's more than that. I can guess at what he is going through. And if I'm right, Larry would want that to be private."

"So it's serious?"

"I'm afraid so, dear. And if we're to be without him for a while, we'll have to improve on the service we did yesterday. Have you got any ideas?"

"I haven't wanted to face it. We'll have to bring in a lot of guests. Celebrities if possible. Maybe lengthen the musical portions." She touched his arm. "We will be relying a lot more on you, Grandpa. Are you up to that?"

"Sure. Just let me know how much time you think you need. Maybe two short segments would be better than one long one."

"Mark doesn't want to air the tape. What do you think?"

Patrick rested his forearms on the table.

"One lie always needs a bigger one to cover it up. Let them see it."

CHAPTER EIGHTEEN

MARK HAD CLOSED SUE'S OFFICE door more energetically than he intended. None of this was her fault. But, damn, Patrick would probably air the show. What did Patrick care about numbers—either dollar amounts or ratings?

Mark had a very clear picture of Patrick preaching in a dusty tent, and knew he had been as happy there as during the years of the successful TV ministry. And he'd be just as happy if it all folded, like that tent, and went away. Somehow, his enjoyment of life had nothing to do with the great freedom that money gave him. Patrick seemed to need none of it, spent none of it that Mark could discern, except for the house—and probably that had been Gillian's project. Other men in Patrick's position had several homes, jet planes, fancy cars. One even had a private island.

Mark entered his own office and saw a detailed note, marked urgent, taped to the sole empty spot on his desk. Theresa had written it. Apparently someone who was in the audience for the taping had a brother who was a reporter. When told about Larry's

The Filigree Cross

performance, the brother had sensed headlines and wanted an interview.

Mark rubbed his forehead and realized he was sweating. He sat down at his desk and dialed the number. Luckily the reporter was inexperienced and easily appeased. Mark convinced him that the message Larry had meant to deliver had been misunderstood because of his style of delivery. "Sometimes that happens," he said, even managing a chuckle. "We prepare something, and it comes out skewed. We just do it over." He told the young man the show would never air; there was no story.

Not until Wednesday, he thought, replacing the receiver. Unless something happened in the next four days to prevent the show from airing, or Larry had a change of heart, by Wednesday night the gravy train would be derailed.

Public relations pieces, press releases and advertisements littered his desk, all of which might have to be changed drastically, but he couldn't do any of that now. He initialed a stack of invoices waiting for his approval and returned a few phone calls, but his mind was stuck on Broadfellow. He wanted nothing more than to wring the man's neck. Finally, in frustration, he pulled his coat from the closet and left.

WIND-DRIVEN SNOW SLAPPED at Mark's face and whipped his coat wide as he stepped outside. The covered walkway between the building and the parking lot was a wind tunnel NASA would envy. But the Mercedes purred to life, and he felt a bit better, anticipating seeing Janet. Then he remembered the time of day. She might well be out shopping or eating, but he could drop by anyway. He had a key. He could at least sit in quiet and enjoy a strong drink by the fire.

But she was home, her cheeks still pink from the cold.

She embraced him in the doorway. "I just got in. What a wonderful surprise. I so seldom get to see you in daylight." She stood at arm's length and appraised him. "And you're actually much better looking than I thought."

Mark grinned. He was never sure how much of what she said was sincere, how much a dig.

She pulled him inside and gestured to the shopping bags on the floor by the sofa. "You can see where I've been."

Apparently she'd left a wide swath at a ritzy boutique. He didn't recognize the name, but its stature was evident from its pink plastic shopping bags with dainty braided leather handles.

She bent over one of the bags, Mark noting the tight, smooth line of her hips curving from that slim waist. She straightened, holding a black sequined dress by its spaghetti straps. As it unfolded from a carefully constructed nest, layers of scented tissue wafted onto the rug. She hugged the dress against her body and gave him the benefit of a few tantalizing hip movements. "Like it?"

Against her creamy skin and brilliant red hair the gown was fabulous. "What's not to like?" He pulled her against him, the dress suspended between them. He pushed back a handful of hair and kissed her neck, taking in her wonderful perfume, somewhere between sweet and earthy. As always, she kissed him eagerly but was careful about the dress. She eased herself back.

The Filigree Cross

"Can't you wait just a moment?" she teased, tracing his lips with a perfect fingernail. She laid the dress over the back of the sofa and returned to him. The cashmere she wore felt like a cloud. Mark closed his eyes and drifted with it.

Hours later they sat in front of the fire, braced by huge cushions, he in his shorts, she in a satin wrap that slipped along her skin, exposing a different part of her body every time she moved.

"I wish it could be like this all the time," he said.

She smiled at him. "I could stand to see more of you." She giggled. Wine made her childlike and he loved it. She ran her toes up his leg. They moved under the hem of his boxers. "Why don't you take these off?"

Mark felt himself flush. In bed he could forget everything, abandon himself completely, but anywhere else he became self-conscious.

"Scaredy-pants." To goad him on, she shrugged and her wrap fell open, exposing her breasts. She loved this teasing and it drove him mad, but he knew from experience that teasing was all it was. She never liked to make love in quick succession. She just wanted him to be always ready.

Janet giggled again and drained her glass. "Another?" she asked, rising languidly to her feet.

Mark wanted desperately to say yes, to stay and let the night come, but he could not, and she knew it.

"You know how I'd love to."

She was pouring her wine. "I know, sweets. It's okay. After all, I didn't even expect you today, so this was special."

She always made it sound like she was the grateful one, when Mark knew he was far more needy than she.

He lived in fear that one day she would tire of him. How many hundreds of men—more powerful, better looking, maybe younger—could step in and make her happy?

SWIRLING SNOW MADE VISIBILITY BAD and Mark cursed at the logjam of cars. He flicked the radio on to get the traffic report. The seven o'clock news came on. Bev and the kids would wait another half hour, then start dinner without him. Then, after the kids were in bed, there would be explanations, recriminations, and lies.

The broad street where their house sat looked even wider with no leaves on the trees lining the road. Worn excuses ran through Mark's head. 'Working late' didn't cut it anymore. Bev had called the office a couple of times to check. Having a drink with his cronies didn't work anymore either—she suggested he invite his friends to the house. His mind was casting about for a new line as he punched the opener and the garage door rose. Bev's car wasn't there. He pulled the Mercedes in and thought for a moment. Had he forgotten some function? Was he supposed to meet them somewhere?

He opened the kitchen door and yelled for the children. The twin boys, aged eleven, usually made enough noise for a troop. And sweet six-year-old Alicia, who loved him to distraction, always dashed, breathless, into his arms. But all was silent. The perfectly clean kitchen table meant dinner was either over or not contemplated. Only a manila envelope with his name hand-written on the outside sat on the polished oak. Mark ripped the envelope open. He lifted out a sheaf of papers. The letterhead read, 'Griffin & Graves, Attorneys at Law, P.C.'

Mark sank into a chair and began to read. He couldn't believe his bad fortune. First Larry jumping ship, now this. Ashamed of himself, his first thought was of Janet, even before thinking about what this meant for his children. He made himself concentrate on them, but realized this would not be a big loss for the boys. Mark had never had time to follow their activities properly. Bev and her folks had always been the ones at the soccer games and band practice and the fundraisers. His boys, Todd and Randy, would be in good hands. Their grandpa was a much better dad than Mark had ever been. But Alicia. She thought her dad was wonderful. A divorce would break her little heart. When did things get so desperate that he was willing to risk losing her?

He loved Bev as much as he was capable of loving anyone. She was a pretty, decent woman who had done nothing to deserve a philandering husband. But Mark's ego demanded more and more attention as he got older, and he had not invested enough in his marriage to assure that he would get that from Bev. So there had followed a half dozen liaisons, none of which mattered to him, until Janet.

And Janet had dollar signs attached to her. Not that she needed anything from Mark. He'd have felt more confident if she did. No, Janet had her own money. But she liked people who also had money, who lived at her level. Because Mark had been struggling to keep up for six months, his credit cards were at the danger point. Now there would be child support and alimony.

He grabbed up the papers, leafed anxiously through them, and found the bottom line. It seemed her lawyer thought Bev would need several years of schooling before she could hope to re-enter the job market. The alimony sum stunned him. Surely, surely, this could not happen. He'd need to get his own attorney. He threw the papers in disarray on the table, called Tech, and climbed back into his car.

MARK SAT, HEAD DOWN, NURSING HIS drink. They were at Dolly's, a first rate bar built in the fifties. Deep banquette seats of quilted maroon leather rose high behind them, allowing some privacy.

Technicolor grabbed Mark's shoulder and gave it a squeeze. "Sorry to hear it. Must have been a shock."

"Hell, yes," Mark blurted. Then he lowered his voice. "She never threatened me, never said a goddamn word about doing this." He paused to pick up his drink. "I don't know what the hell I was thinking. She's not a stupid woman."

"Does she know about Janet?"

"From the terms of the settlement, I'd say she feels she's on solid ground."

"Maybe it will blow over," Tech suggested. "Maybe she just wants to make a point."

Mark considered this. No, it was not like Bev to play games. And she'd gone to a lot of expense already, just getting the papers prepared.

Tech had experience with the subject. "Well, she'll only get half, regardless of the issues."

Mark scoffed. "Most of it is hers. Her folks gave us half the cost of the house. My car isn't nearly paid for. Maybe she'll let me keep the boat since she hates it,

The Filigree Cross

and I can sell that for a ten-thousand-dollar loss. Financially I'm screwed. There's no other way to put it."

Technicolor motioned to the cocktail waitress for another round. "Look, I'd like to offer you some help, but who knows what's going to happen to both our jobs if Larry doesn't come back."

Mark sat up straight and looked Tech in the eyes. "Hey, I'm not asking for anything from you. Nothing like that." He paused. "But, you know, I do think the ministry owes us. The money rolls in like the tide, every day, every day. There's tons of it. Larry himself said I've been doing a good job. And you work unbelievable hours because they don't want too many people knowing the details. Why shouldn't we get our share?"

Tech spun the ice cubes in his empty glass.

Mark shifted a little closer to his friend and lowered his voice to a whisper. "What became of that extra bank account?"

"It's still there."

"How much is in it?"

"Three hundred and thirty thousand, plus. Why?"

Mark's face fell. He'd hoped for more. Half of that, if Tech would consider splitting it two ways, would keep him for a year or two.

"What would we have to do to get our hands on it?"

Technicolor hesitated. "Not a good idea, Mark. They call that embezzlement."

"Hey, you're a genius. You could do it."

"It would be complicated. We would have to set up a real charity, give some of the money away. Very risky."

Mark saw the pot dwindling. "What about auditors?"

"We've just finished an audit. Won't have a thorough one for another two years. Without Larry, the ministry won't last that long. I've got feelers out. You should, too."

"Yeah." No new job would pay him what he was getting now. "About the other, though, what are the chances?"

"Maybe it could be done. I don't really want to think about it," Tech said. "I wish we'd never set the account up in the first place. Now, I'm not sure how to put it right."

Mark tossed a twenty on the table. "Look, thanks for meeting me. I really appreciate it."

"No problem. Take it easy."

Mark turned at the doorway and went back to the table. "Did you know the Brannigans had a daughter?"

"I think I heard something once. Must be Sue's mother."

"Ever met her?"

Tech shook his head.

"What's her name?"

"I don't know."

"Doesn't that seem odd? That we've never heard a word about her? Or Sue's father for that matter."

"It has always seemed like an unwritten rule not to ask. Does that bother you?"

"Yeah, it bugs me," Mark said, moving away again.

The Filigree Cross

"You're just in a pissy mood," Tech said. "Tomorrow will look better."

MARK HEADED BACK TO THE HOUSE. He desperately wanted to see Janet, but knew better. The last thing she would like on her doorstep was a newly divorced man with money problems, and he didn't have the gumption, right now, to fake it.

Sunday morning he woke early. The last night spent in his own bed left him groggy from too little sleep and too much worry. Tumbled with a thousand other thoughts, Janet's face and body had recurred often, and he woke wanting her. Steeped in desire, he allowed himself a moment's irrationality. Could she love him in spite of his money problems? A harsh grunt burst from his throat, startling in the quiet of the empty house. He mentally slapped himself awake. Come on, man. Be resourceful.

Overlying his worries all night was the mystery of Brannigan's unknown daughter. The Brannigans seemed open, and guileless, and a very close family. That made it all the more perplexing. Surely, there must be some tragedy involved—Sue's parents killed in a terrible accident, perhaps. But even that would hardly be something to ignore so pointedly.

Mark replayed the words Larry had used in the service. "Lovely daughter," he had said. Had she been a romantic interest of Larry's? Suddenly adrenaline made his arms itch and his neck tense. Could Sue be Larry's daughter? Her age was about right. Why would that have to be a secret? There was a skeleton in someone's closet. He wondered about the monetary value of its staying there.

CHAPTER NINETEEN

A SLIT OF SUN CUTTING across his pillow finally woke Larry at ten o'clock Sunday morning. After staying awake for thirty-odd hours following the disastrous taping, he had finally fallen into a dreamless stupor. For a few moments he felt like his former self, until memory caught up. The gnawing hollowness in his stomach had nothing to do with lack of food. He saw his life stretching out before him, a lonely road without guideposts.

He pushed himself slowly to a sitting position as if he were rising out of sludge. He rubbed at his face and eyes. He'd been honest with Sue; without preaching he felt he didn't exist. And it seemed preaching was no longer an option.

Ever since reading Gillian's letter, he'd been listening to himself with new ears. He didn't want to go to his own grave feeling his life had been a sham. Where he would go from here, what he would do, were total mysteries. He had no training for anything else. There was money enough that he could do nothing at all if he chose; but that would hardly redeem his life.

The Filigree Cross

He opened the drapes and let the sun blind him. Its warmth almost felt like a blessing, an odd thought. After the gray days, which reminded everyone that full winter skulked just around the corner, the blue sky seemed very precious. Gillian had loved crisp days like this, he thought. And Fiona would, too. If he could talk her into it again, he would take Fiona out for a drive. That would take care of the first day of the rest of his life.

He called Patrick. The phone rang several times.

Larry felt immense guilt about so many things, including all the people who would be out of work if the church did not survive. But his first concern was leaving Patrick and Sue in such a spot. Patrick could probably have carried the church years ago, but, in his present state of health, returning to such a schedule would take an awful toll.

Patrick answered, a little breathless.

"Good morning," Larry said, unsure of his status. He'd been a hermit for two days, turning away everyone's well-meant advances. But he should have known better than to doubt Patrick; the man's voice was all-welcoming.

"You sound a lot better, son. Come on up and have breakfast with Sue and me."

"I'd like that, but I'm going to pick up Fiona and take her for a drive. I thought I'd bring her back to the house afterwards, maybe for dinner."

"Great," Patrick exclaimed. "I'll have Sue get a cake; we'll make it a party. The painters just finished with the study door. It is now turquoise with sunflowers and daisies and butterflies. It will make a perfect surprise."

"You painted that beautiful door?" Larry said, astounded. All the doors at the house were custom-carved in solid walnut.

"No. I replaced it. I think she'll be delighted. I know it makes *me* smile. You two have a good day, and we'll be looking for you."

DURING THE NOW FAMILIAR ROUTE to Golden Hills, Larry mentally thanked Gillian for asking him to do this. Visiting Fiona was the only self-sacrificing thing he could remember doing in his life, the only thing he did for no reward other than a smile.

Fiona had her hair in two braids tied with yellow ribbons. As their eyes met he thought he saw a flicker of sadness. Did her face relax from its childlike grin? Did he hear a sharp intake of her breath? Larry stared into her eyes, looking for the real Fiona. However, she spun around, making her skirt fly out, and giggled.

Larry's heart sank. Each time he saw her he had to readjust his thinking. This new Fiona was a warm, unique individual. Even though she did not bear any emotional resemblance to the intuitive creature she was born to be, he must accept her for now.

"Have you been dancing?" he asked, handing over the cookies. She nodded, pointing to the window. "It's like summer again."

"I've got a wonderful surprise for today."

Her eyes shone as she searched his face. "We'll see the geese again?" He had taken her on a very quick trip to a city park the week before, and they were lucky to see some late-migrating Canada geese.

"Better than that."

The Filigree Cross

"Nothing's better than that," she said, very sure of herself. Larry saw that his carved duck sat in a position of importance on her bedside table.

"We're going to drive out into the country and breath all that wonderful air."

"How far?" Her voice held apprehension.

"We could drive for a couple of hours, have some tea or lunch. Then I'd like to take you to see your father. He misses you."

She bit at her bottom lip.

"What are you worried about?"

"Will I like the country?"

"I'm sure you will. There will be thousands of trees. Lots of lakes and birds; we might even see a deer."

This ignited her. "A deer? Really?"

Larry regretted his words. Were there any deer within two hours of the city? He had no idea. Perhaps he'd have to default to the zoo. If there were deer there.

"We'll see one if we're really lucky," he said.

"Well, I'm really lucky. Let's go."

As he drove, Larry racked his brain for a destination. Recreation had always meant a trip to Barbados with a new acquaintance or a short European jaunt. Then he remembered a visit to Starved Rock State Park he had taken a few years back with a lady friend. He headed west on Interstate 80.

As the suburbs turned to countryside, Fiona rolled down her window. She stuck her hand out, turning it to feel the wind on every surface. Then she undid her braids and ran her fingers through her hair, lifting it so it flew. She leaned her head out the window, her breath catching in the force of the air.

Larry's breath caught, too. He recalled her at sixteen, as they traveled the roads that first summer, catching raindrops on her tongue from the open window of the Oldsmobile. He felt himself at the wheel of that old car, remembered complaining about its condition and a hundred other minor things. How could he have been so stupid not to realize the joy of those times? But he had been so eager to give it up that he talked Patrick into staying in Terre Haute. If they had kept moving Fiona would not have been on the highway the day she was attacked. If they had kept moving she might be sitting beside him, just as she was now, but as his wife. They might be poor, he would certainly not be famous. He would trade it all in the blink of an eye.

Lost in memories, he almost missed the signs for the park. Just in time he turned south on 178 to Utica, and soon they were at the Illinois and Michigan Canal. On an impulse he parked in the visitor area and took Fiona to where they could watch the operation of the locks.

"You see how the river is lower on that side than it is over here?" he asked, pointing to their left and their right. She nodded. The lower lock was almost filled with boats—tugboats, pleasure craft, merchant ships. A bell clanged a warning and a wall slid into place behind the boats. Fiona watched intently.

"Now they'll fill the lock with water and raise the boats up to the level of the river over here."

The boats bobbed and bumped as they were raised up. When they reached the level of the river once

The Filigree Cross

again, the wall in front of them opened, and they were released into their journeys.

Fiona's hand was on her cheek, her eyes glued to the action. As the boats dispersed at various speeds with a wide range of noises, she looked up at Larry, her eyes shining.

"Have I been here before?"

Larry looked at her intently, not daring to hope. He'd never heard her refer to her past in any way. Had she seen the locks as a youngster?

"Do you remember this?"

She didn't answer immediately, and he held his breath as he waited.

But she just shrugged, and then the thought seemed to vanish. She took a deep breath of the air and wrinkled her nose. "Gasoline," she said. "Could we go on a boat?"

He nodded absently. "Sure. Some day soon."

As they drove into the park and approached the lodge, Larry remembered the large chain-saw sculptures of bald eagles and black bear cubs that led up to the its entrance. As expected, Fiona gasped with delight and wanted to touch them. He parked the car and they walked among the animals.

If she felt insecure so far from the clinic she hid it. Perhaps she was doing so well because they'd been encountering things that grabbed her attention. Wondering if she would be able to handle a crowd of people, Larry suggested they go into the gift shop. Fiona forgot herself completely and fell in love with the huge artificial tree that loomed inside, decorated with white lights. Its limbs stretched out over the shelves of gifts. Passing the T-shirts, Indian artifacts, and crafts, she picked out postcard pictures of the sculptures and one with a photo of Cascade Falls.

"Can we go here today?" she asked, holding it up to him. She had certainly overcome her fear of travel.

Larry turned it over. The falls were a few miles south in Matthiesen State Park. He decided to keep something for another time, and since she had the photo it would give her something to look forward to.

"Not today. Maybe next week. How about some lunch?"

Larry had no appetite, but Fiona enjoyed her sandwich and ordered caramel pecan cheesecake. While they waited for her dessert, Larry asked her why she was so quiet.

"I was thinking about those boats. I remember where I saw them before."

Larry forced a casual tone. "Do you remember how old you were?"

She giggled. "As old as I am now, silly. There's a picture of them in one of the books in my room."

Larry's stomach turned over as though he had eaten something bad. So this was his punishment: to always think she would get better, to be unable to face the facts, to be disappointed every day for the rest of his life.

They drove through the park and stopped when they had a good view of the sandstone butte that was Starved Rock. The river curled, dark blue, around its circular base. The rock rose steeply a hundred and twenty-five feet from the water. Trees crowned its flat surface.

The Filigree Cross

Larry told Fiona about the Indians who had starved on its top rather than face capture by a warrior band down below.

She frowned. "Were the white men after them?"

"No. It was another Indian tribe."

As they walked back to the car, Fiona said, "Those Indians died slowly."

"Probably."

She put her hand in his.

Larry asked, "Does that frighten you?"

"A little," she said. "But I feel safe with you."

DINNER AT THE MANSION went smoothly, though Fiona had destroyed her appetite. When she came upon the painted door she clapped her hands, grinned and hugged Patrick. Her enthusiasm was contagious. Larry watched her innocent delight infuse all of them. Even Sue, who tempered her reactions to her mother, laughed freely.

Later, Sue's eyes lingered on Larry and he could read her thoughts as clearly as if she were speaking. *She is lovely, she is happy, but we can't keep her like this.*

CHAPTER TWENTY

ON WEDNESDAY NIGHT Maureen Cameron finished her dinner and sat eagerly in front of her television set. Finally it was time for the Church of God's Love. The voices of that wonderful choir swelled, expanding Maureen's heart, as she settled back into her chair. With pride, she pictured Johnny somewhere behind the scenes helping to put the service on the air. Maybe Johnny had been able to talk to Reverend Broadfellow by now. She hoped so. What Johnny needed in his life was a strong man to look up to.

When Larry Broadfellow came on stage and made his first comment about having no words at his disposal, Maureen chuckled. But as he continued in that same vein, her smile faded. She saw something haunting in his eyes. Even his body seemed awkward; he normally moved with such grace. By the time he began talking about the paucity of deposits in his heavenly account, tears were streaming down her cheeks. When he hugged Reverend Brannigan and said goodbye, she sobbed aloud, clutching at the front of her blouse.

The Filigree Cross

As soon as she could get herself together, she called her grandson. "What happened, Johnny? What happened to Reverend Broadfellow?"

Johnny's voice sounded old. "No one seems to know, Gram. I wish I'd told you the truth, but I kept hoping that they wouldn't air this show, that you might not have to see it. There are a lot of rumors, like he's sick or in some kind of trouble."

"Oh, dear. Did you ever get to talk to him?"

"No. I saw him just before that taping, but right afterwards he practically ran from the building. Billy Sills said no one on the crew has seen him."

"I'm just sick about this. He must be suffering so. Isn't there any way you can find out what the problem is? Go see him, Johnny. Just to find out if he's okay. Could you do that?"

"Gosh, Gram. I told you, no one has seen him. Why would he talk to me?"

"Maybe he'd remember you from the Minneapolis show. You could remind him."

"Gram, you just don't understand. Mr. Broadfellow's a big star. This is a huge operation. I'm nobody here."

"I know you can find a way, Johnny. Please try for me."

SUE TURNED TO THE HUNDRED details yet to be clarified before the day's rehearsal, but it was impossible to read her notes through building tears. She slapped her notebook on the desk and grabbed a tissue. Jimmy Makaani had just left her office after telling her he wanted to return to Hawaii. His family's church had been trying to bring him home for a year. It was growing, they were raising funds for a new building, and they needed his help. Jimmy felt that with Larry leaving the ministry this was a good time. He had asked Sue to marry him. But how could she leave her mother or her ailing grandfather? Especially now, with his church in such disarray. Leaving was simply not an option now, much as her heart longed for things to be otherwise, and she feared Jimmy would go without her.

After a few minutes, Sue dried her eyes and returned to the tasks before her. Her door must have been ajar because, at the same time as she heard the knock, someone called out, "Ms. Brannigan?" The door swung part way open and Johnny Cameron's face appeared.

"Hello, Johnny. Do you need something?"

He entered hesitantly. "It's not for me. Is this a bad time?"

She straightened her shoulders. "Come on in. Just a hitch in my day. Any problems?"

He took a few steps into the room. "Well, it's my grandmother, really. I know a lot of people must be worried about Reverend Broadfellow. My grandmother loves him; she really does. It's making her very anxious, not knowing. I was hoping you could tell me something to tell her. It wouldn't have to go any further."

"I know the rumors," she said finally. "But he's not ill. Would that satisfy your grandmother?"

"She wants to know if he's coming back. I really think it will make her sick if he doesn't."

Sue gazed past his shoulder. Here was an innocent kid asking the sixty-four-thousand-dollar question.

The Filigree Cross

Johnny represented the thousands upon thousands who'd written and called needing the same information. Why should she be the one to have to face him, or them? Larry is the one who should shoulder this. He should have to face everyone he had disappointed. For the first time she felt anger toward Larry.

"Johnny, would you be willing to do me a favor if I do you one?"

"Of course, Ms. Brannigan. I'd do you one any time."

"I'd like Larry to talk to you. I think you represent the millions of people he's forgotten, but who wait moment by moment to hear from him again."

She walked closer to Johnny, holding his gaze. "But if I ask him to meet with you I know he'll turn us down. What I propose is that you go to see him, pretending you have an appointment that I had set up. I'll claim later that I forgot to tell him about it."

Johnny frowned.

She pressed further. "It isn't much of a trick against Mr. Broadfellow. He could still not talk to you if he chose."

LARRY PUSHED HIS PLATE AWAY. Sue had insisted on bringing him a full evening meal, but his appetite had been satisfied with the first few bites. She had been quiet when she delivered the tray, saying only that the auditions of several guests had gone well. For once she hadn't tried to coax him to come to the mansion. On Sunday, with Fiona along, it had been easy. All the attention was focused on her. But to face

Sue and Patrick for an hour or more over a dinner table was something he couldn't imagine.

He had come to recognize yet another void in his life. He had never admitted to himself how much the audience meant to him. He missed the applause, the shouts of joy, the satisfaction of knowing he'd brought them to a place of happiness.

A knock on the door startled him. As he opened it, a young man stepped into the pool of outside light, his hands clasped behind his back.

"Reverend Broadfellow, my name is Johnny Cameron. You probably don't remember me." His hands moved to his sides, fingering the edge of this jacket.

"Actually, you do look familiar. But I've forgotten where we met."

"Minneapolis. My gram and I were down front."

Larry remembered all too well.

The young man's brow furrowed and he began to explain further. "Now I work with Billy Sills. Sue Brannigan hired me."

"Of course," Larry said politely. "I know who you are. Is there something you need?" Larry realized he was being rude not inviting him in, but he didn't really want any company.

"I need to talk to you. Ms. Brannigan said she'd call ahead and let you know I was coming." The young man blushed almost scarlet when he said this.

Johnny Cameron didn't look like a liar. But Larry had seen Sue just an hour before, and she'd said nothing. She was much too efficient for a slip like that. What was it about these Cameron people, always catching him off guard?

The Filigree Cross

He'd decided to simply send the young man away when Johnny continued. "My gram is making herself sick, Reverend Broadfellow, worrying about you. What you said on that last show scared her. She said if God had turned his back on you, he sure couldn't care too much about someone like her."

Larry's shoulders slumped, then he stepped back into the house. "Come in," he said.

Johnny accepted a cup of coffee with lots of cream and sugar and wrapped his hands around its heat. After the eruption of words at the door, he seemed to have lost his momentum.

Larry tried to relax into his chair. He had no idea what to tell this young man and his grandmother, but perhaps he owed them something.

"I'm sorry about that service in Minneapolis," he began. "It must have disappointed your grandmother."

"Oh, no! She thought it was wonderful. She was so grateful to you. It was a wonderful thing to have happen to her. And to think it only happened because I was so scared."

"Scared? What do you mean?"

Johnny beamed. "You don't know how happy I was to get that two thousand dollars back."

Larry sat up straight. "What two thousand dollars?"

Johnny hesitated. "Oh, I thought you knew."

"Tell me."

"Well, Gram sent twenty dollars for Mrs. Brannigan's memorial. She expected a special note or something, and when she didn't get it she thought she hadn't sent enough money. So, without me knowing about it, she mailed a two thousand dollar check."

"She sent the first twenty dollars for Mrs. Brannigan's memorial? Didn't she get that back as well?"

"Nope. Just the usual computer thank you. That's what disturbed her—it didn't say anything about a memorial for Mrs. Brannigan." Johnny added quickly, "Of course, we don't want the twenty dollars back."

Larry's thoughts ran to Tech. Money for Gillian's memorial not returned. Where did it go? But he didn't want to convey any of this concern to his visitor. He smiled. "Well, it worked out in the end, then."

"Oh, yeah. Perfectly," Johnny assured him, settling back into his chair.

Johnny seemed to be waiting for the explanation of Larry's departure.

"How old are you Johnny?"

"Eighteen."

"I went into the navy when I was eighteen."

"Did you like it, sir?"

"First, please, don't call me sir. The navy was okay, except that's where I learned to drink." Maybe he could shock this young man, tumble himself from the pedestal Johnny's grandmother had put him on. "For the next eight years, that was all I did."

Johnny nodded and looked down; he was anything but shocked. "I know all about that. My mom can't stop." Then he looked into Larry's eyes. "How did you stop? Was that when you found God?"

Oh, sweet Jesus. The words echoed in Larry's ears. Sweet Jesus had been the favorite expression of the plumber, Mr. Burns, at the orphanage in Madison. What took him back there? Maybe this young man's

The Filigree Cross

innocence. "Do you think people find God when they're in trouble, Johnny?"

"Not always. My mom is in real trouble and I don't think she'll ever find Him. I think God finds some people and not others."

"Why not everyone?"

Johnny shook his head slowly, then lowered it.

Larry was astonished to see a tear plop onto the table. Johnny quickly covered it with his sleeve, but did not raise his head.

Larry reached over the table and touched the young man's arm. "What's the matter, son?"

Words burst from his chest. "I've hardly slept since your visit to Minneapolis. Something took hold of me that night. I'm afraid God is trying to reach me. That's why I came to work for you, Reverend Broadfellow. I admire you so much and I think God wants me to serve Him, and I don't know what to do. And now, if you're leaving—" Johnny put his hands over his face and sobbed.

Larry stared, dumbfounded. What next? He rose and paced the room. Then he moved around the table and patted Johnny's shoulder.

"Take it easy, son. Take it easy."

Slowly the heaving in Johnny's shoulders became less pronounced, and he calmed down. Larry refilled the boy's coffee cup and urged him to drink.

Johnny wiped at his face with a sleeve and looked up, mortified. "I'm sorry. I don't know what happened."

Larry hated himself for skirting around Johnny's dilemma, but how could he help this young man when he, himself, was so disconnected from the Lord. Larry had never experienced anything remotely like the calling Johnny seemed to fear. "Perhaps you're tired," he said. "Worried too much about your mother and your grandmother. Young men your age sometimes get pretty emotional about things."

Johnny nodded.

"I'm curious, though. What happened that made you feel God is calling you to His work?"

Johnny spoke in fits and starts. "I'm not normal. No, that's not the right word. I don't fit in with people my age, and yet I'm not lonely. Or, wasn't until very recently. Now I feel empty sometimes, and so full I could break open other times. It's a restlessness that stays with me day and night. But I've never been religious. Why would God want me?"

Indeed, Larry thought. How does He choose? Why would He give words to a someone who didn't even believe what came out of his own mouth?

Johnny was staring at him. Larry realized he'd forgotten his guest.

"Johnny, I don't think I'm the person to help you with this. I was never ordained."

Johnny's eyes widened. "You weren't?"

Larry picked up his coffee cup and moved toward his study. "Why don't we sit in here? It's more comfortable."

Larry lit the gas fireplace and they sat on either side. Both were quiet for several minutes, Johnny's eyes taking in all the carved birds.

Then Johnny spoke. Larry knew he was trying not to be rude, but was too curious to let it go. "If you're not a reverend or anything, how come you preach?"

The Filigree Cross

Larry stretched his long legs then drew them under him again. "It started very innocently, accidentally almost. It just grew."

Johnny's voice became animated. "How old were you when you started? Have you always worked with the Church of God's Love, or did you start somewhere else?"

There was such admiration and anticipation in the boy's eyes that Larry could hardly meet his gaze. If this young man thought Larry was someone to emulate, he'd better set him straight.

Skipping the early years, he began, "I met Reverend Brannigan and his family when I was twenty-six." He put his hand on his chest, rubbing in wide, slow circles. His voice became rough-edged. "I worked for them," he said. "Reverend Brannigan was a traveling tent minister. I did odd jobs, anything from raising the tent to taking the laundry to the Wash-and-Go. It was a truly wonderful summer, that first one." Larry studied the fire. The memories were too sharp. Suddenly he wanted to be alone.

"I'm sure my history is boring. Why don't we call it an evening?"

"Oh, it's not boring at all," Johnny said. "I'd love to know how you got started. Maybe I could do something like you did."

In that young face, so eager in the slanting firelight, Larry saw a boy stretching to his destiny, and for the first time believed that perhaps it was more than a youthful fantasy.

"No, you must never do anything the way I did it. If you truly feel a calling, you must do as Reverend Brannigan did, through education. Learn the gospel, and history. Read and reread the Bible, study the meditations of those who went before. You need to build such a firm foundation that nothing can ever shake it."

"But you didn't study for all those years, and you reach millions of people who love you—"

Larry stood quickly, stopping Johnny's words. His voice was hard, impatient. "I've given you my best advice, Johnny. That's all I can do." He moved briskly down the hall.

Johnny leaped to his feet and grabbed his jacket from the kitchen chair. As Larry opened the door Johnny ran into the night, not looking back.

Larry watched him for a few seconds, then slammed the door. All he wanted was to step down from the ministry, admit his defeat, and go quietly away. Was Johnny's visit a precursor of things to come—people refusing to let him go, picking at him, dissecting his motives? If not for Fiona, he'd leave the country and let them stew in their own imaginings.

LARRY TOSSED IN A FITFUL SLEEP. A collage of memories and fantasies raced through his brain. When, in his nightmare, he reached for Fiona and took her in a romantic embrace, her innocent eyes searched his, begging for understanding. Regardless, he pressed his lips to hers. At their touch he woke suddenly with a roar, throwing the covers off.

"God, oh God!" he shouted. His breath was pumping his chest like a bellows. He shook his head. She was still a child, one who trusted him implicitly.

Disgusted with himself, Larry stood in a raging hot shower until her face disappeared from behind his eyes

The Filigree Cross

and his skin turned red. When he turned off the faucet he heard a firm banging at his front door. "Larry, Larry," a man was shouting.

He grabbed a towel. As he moved to the door, he saw the mantel clock, its numerals glowing in the dark: 2:30 a.m.

Simon, Patrick's groundskeeper, wearing a coat thrown over night clothes, gazed at him sorrowfully. Larry gasped at the cold air. "Come in," he said, backing away to close the door.

"No. We've been trying to call you. Patrick has had another stroke, or a heart attack. He's on the way to the hospital. Sue's in the ambulance with him."

CHAPTER TWENTY-ONE

"WILL YOU SLEEP FOR A WHILE?" Larry asked Patrick. He needed to do the same. Larry, Sue and Jimmy Makaani had walked hospital corridors for two days, almost around the clock. Now Patrick was back at the house, settled in his own bed. Bottles of pills covered the top of a small table at his bedside. But Larry doubted their promise. Patrick's eyes said he was ready, maybe eager, to leave this world.

Patrick turned his head slowly, his breathing shallow, his voice almost a whisper. "I'd like to see Fiona. Very soon, son."

Larry's heart gripped. He patted the old man's hand. "I'll go get her."

Larry moved downstairs, then hesitated when he saw Sue sitting in the living room, head down. Jimmy stood behind her chair rubbing her shoulders. "Will you please rest now?" Jimmy begged her.

Jimmy helped her to her feet and took her in his arms. Larry saw her collapse into him. The weight of all the losses she'd suffered in her short life seemed to pull at her shoulders. Her mother's retreat from life, then Gillian's death, now Patrick. And she would be

The Filigree Cross

losing the work that had given her so much fulfillment. She looked as though she couldn't handle one more thing.

As he passed the open doorway, Larry heard Jimmy say, "You're going to take one of those sleeping pills whether you want to or not."

LARRY DROVE CAREFULLY, knowing exhaustion was affecting his reaction time. Beside him, Fiona kept lacing and unlacing her fingers. What would Patrick's imminent death mean to her? He explained that Patrick was sick, that she might not like the way he looked. "He's pale and weak, but he wants very much to see you." She didn't reply.

"YOU'RE MY LITTLE GIRL, you know," Patrick said when she was seated on the edge of his mattress.

She nodded and took his hand. Larry sighed with relief.

"Do you remember our green and white striped tent?" Patrick asked. "We had wonderful summers, didn't we?" A smile spread across his face and he turned to gaze up at the ceiling. Then his eyes fluttered closed and he suddenly fell asleep.

Gloria, the housekeeper, tip-toed into the room. She whispered to Larry that there was a man, Mark McLaren, waiting downstairs to see him.

Surely Mark hadn't chosen this time to whine any more about Larry coming back to the ministry. As he rose to leave the room, Fiona reached for him.

"You stay here. I'll be right back."

MARK WAS PACING THE FOYER, clearly nervous. In one hand he held a manila envelope.

"How is Patrick?" Mark asked.

"Very weak." Larry leaned against the banister. He couldn't remember ever being so tired.

"What will happen to the ministry?" Mark asked.

"It's over."

"But you could—"

In frustration Larry banged a fist on the carved wood. "Mark, it's no good. Give it up. You don't understand." A headache began to pound at his temples.

"Look, I know it's a bad time, but I want to talk to you in private."

"Not today. Not this week. We've got enough going on." Larry turned to go back up the stairs.

Mark grabbed his arm. "You have to talk to me, Larry."

Larry shrugged Mark's hand away. "What the hell do you mean, I have to talk to you. See yourself out."

Larry had one foot on the first step when Mark's voice stopped him.

"I know why Patrick had to leave his first church."

Larry turned. "How do you happen to know about that?"

"We need to find some privacy," Mark said.

As they headed for his house, Larry's mind raced. In all these years he had never heard a whisper about Patrick's past. Why now?

Once in his office Larry confronted Mark. "What possessed you to dig into Patrick's history, Mark? Because I know this couldn't have just landed in your lap."

The Filigree Cross

Mark put on a nervous half-smile. "Actually, you got me interested, when you made that last speech about the church's humble beginnings. I think you slipped up for once in your life."

"What do you mean, slipped up?"

"You mentioned Brannigan's daughter." Mark paused. "I wondered where she was, who she was. No one in the ministry seemed to know."

"But, now, you do."

Mark tossed the envelope he'd been carrying on the desk. "I know it all, Larry. I started out to find the daughter but a little research gave me much more than I ever expected. I know about the sexual abuse charges against Patrick. I even know who the boy was."

Larry wanted to reach out and strike the smirk off Mark's face. But he needed to know what his game was. "Well, you know what kind of a man Patrick is. You must realize that was a total misinterpretation of events."

"I'm not sure how well any of us knows each other."

"I'm getting a damn good lesson right now," Larry countered. He stared into Mark's eyes until Mark had to look away. "I always thought you were a self-centered s.o.b., but I sure didn't realize you were pure scum. What are you after?"

"I need money."

"You always need money."

"Real money. I'm in a personal mess. I need it now."

"And you came here, today, to threaten a dying man? You're a real case, McLaren."

"Look, Patrick doesn't need to know anything about this."

Larry's voice rose. "And I know why you had to come when he's on his deathbed. Because after he's gone, you've got no leverage, you sick bastard."

Unfazed, Mark took a few steps toward Larry. "At first I thought you and the daughter, Fiona, had been married, and maybe you'd had a child, Sue. But why would that be such a secret? My guess is Sue's illegitimate."

Larry felt his heart crack, hearing this cretin talking so callously about the two women he loved most in the world. He aimed a fist at Mark's jaw. Mark ducked Larry's punch, lunged forward and pinned Larry back against his desk.

Larry realized that Mark's strength, combined with his own fatigue, meant a fight could end only one way. Twisting away from Mark's hold, he saw, over Mark's shoulder, Fiona standing in the open doorway, her hand to her mouth.

When their eyes met, she ran forward and grabbed Mark's shoulders, trying to pull him off of Larry. Without seeing who it was, Mark shoved an elbow back sharply, smashing Fiona in the face. She fell onto the floor, crying out in pain.

The men immediately broke from one another. Larry bent over her and saw blood tracking her cheeks. He pried her hands from her face to see the damage. A broken nose, at least. When she looked up he saw terror in her eyes, so raw it turned him cold. "Fiona, Fiona," he shouted over her cries, "It's all right."

She wrenched one hand free of his grasp and scraped his face with her nails. "Get away, get away!"

The Filigree Cross

A guttural moan began low in her throat and grew to a gut-wrenching cry for her mother. The intensity of her plea filled the room with unspeakable sorrow. Larry released her arms and backed away from her prone and shaking body.

Fiona groped to her feet and ran toward the door. Larry took chase and wrapped his long arms around her and held her. She flung her head wildly, moaning and crying out.

MARK STOOD, STUNNED. This was Fiona. She appeared to be reliving the horror of her attack—the attack his researched newspaper clippings had described only as a gruesome act. He realized it had been so much more. He thought of his own little Alicia and what he would do to any man who caused her pain.

"Call 911!" Larry shouted, bringing Mark out of himself.

Mark made the call, then caught up with Larry who was carrying Fiona to the main house.

BY THE TIME LARRY GOT FIONA inside, her strength had waned and she no longer fought. Larry settled her gently on the sofa and she immediately tucked herself into a fetal position, her moans steeped in hopelessness. Larry had seen the real Fiona for a few minutes. But now she seemed to be drifting into sleep, and Larry feared she would relapse into that safe cocoon.

He pulled her to a sitting position and shook her.

"Fiona, don't go to sleep. Tell me what's happening."

She cringed away from him. Her eyes fluttered open. She searched his face. He saw the fright turn to confusion as she looked around the room, then back to him.

"Larry, oh, Larry," she murmured.

He pulled her into his arms, stroking her head. "Tell me, please. Tell me everything."

She clung to him, sobbing, until the ambulance arrived.

As the paramedics carried her to the vehicle, Larry moved beside them, calling back to Mark. "Call the clinic—Golden Hills. Have Dr. Freidman meet us." Mark nodded, moving toward the phone. "Sue's getting some badly-needed rest. Can I trust you to stay here with Patrick and keep your damned mouth shut?"

"Of course, Larry. I'm really sorry, about everything."

"You'd better bloody well hope she gets well because nothing else is going keep me from killing you."

TWO HOURS LATER MARK sat in his office, an open bottle of whiskey on his desk. Sometimes he used booze to soften the edges, but two quick swallows had served to sharpen his mind. He rubbed both hands roughly through his hair. The entire affair at Larry's house and at the mansion had been a disaster. At the time Jimmy Makaani relieved him, there was still no news from the clinic. Mark recalled Fiona's awful cries and a tremor shook him. To think his actions had caused such pain.

What had he expected when he confronted Larry? That Larry would simply capitulate and hand him money? His desperation had led to a degradation he'd never felt before. How could he have debased himself over money? Money to impress Janet. Why had that seemed more important than being with his own children, especially Alicia. She would be missing him.

One by one he picked up the newspaper articles that he'd culled during his intensive search. They disclosed the charges against Patrick, a story about his poor tent ministry, then Fiona Brannigan's sexual assault, and the discovery that the attacker was a victim of child abuse. He balled them all into a wrinkled mass and tossed them in the waste basket. In concert, the stories added up to depravity. Dissected, they told of individuals struggling with the hand they'd been dealt. His own problems were insignificant in comparison. He tossed the bottle on top of the clippings. Then, thinking better of leaving it there, he retrieved it and stuck it in the pocket of his coat.

He slammed the door behind him and, as he swung down the hallway, the bottle fell from his pocket and shattered. Mark cursed.

"Mark?"

He spun around. "Theresa, who can I get to clean up this mess?"

"I'll call someone if you like."

"Would you? I really need to get moving."

CHAPTER TWENTY-TWO

LARRY'S LEGS HUNG OVER THE END of the green vinyl couch in the hospital waiting room. Though he could not sleep, his body ached so badly he had been forced to lie down. When Dr. Freidman approached, Larry stood on wobbly legs, anxious for a report.

"She's doing very well," the doctor said. "Wonderfully."

"What do you mean?"

"She relived her attack during her struggle, and she realizes that she has survived it. Perhaps that is what is allowing her to speak of it now. This is the very breakthrough we've needed."

Larry's hope must have registered plainly on his face because the doctor immediately couched his words. "Dealing with those memories is going to be incredibly painful, very difficult, but she's facing up to them. She's no longer blocking it out. Given lots of time and therapy, I don't see why she couldn't recover fully."

The Filigree Cross

Larry pressed his palms to his eyes, blocking tears. Dr. Freidman put an arm around his shoulders. "You need some rest. Why not go on home?"

But Larry could not leave. After Dr. Freidman departed, he lay motionless on the waiting room couch in a limbo of exhaustion and emotional turmoil. An irrational thought ran continually through his mind. *Her recovery is my reward for stepping down, proof I did the right thing.* He knew it was incredibly vain, but if God hadn't chosen this timing for a reason, then all was random—and to what purpose?

Thirty minutes later Dr. Freidman entered the room again. "You still awake?"

"I know I need to sleep, but I just can't."

"We can fix that."

Dr. Freidman asked a nurse to locate a spare cot for Larry and give him a shot. Then he slept almost around the clock. As soon as he woke he asked to see Fiona, but she was resting. He left her a note saying he'd be back in the morning and went home to Patrick.

SUE HUGGED HIM THE MOMENT he entered the house. "Isn't it fantastic?" she said. "I still can't believe it."

"Then you've seen her?" Larry asked.

"While you were asleep, very briefly. She seemed confused and withdrawn. I was disappointed at first, but Dr. Freidman explained that we need to be patient. She's been in almost a vacuum all these years, and is overwhelmed trying to grasp the loss of her life. But talking to her was more like talking to an adult, she's very different."

"How much does Patrick know about it?"

"I simply told him she was getting better. He didn't seem surprised, just happy at the news." Sue paused. "I've brought in a full-time nurse."

"Is he getting worse?"

Sue nodded. "I don't think we can leave him alone for a minute. He's so terribly weak."

LARRY FOUND PATRICK not lying down, but sitting, propped by pillows, a Bible in his lap.

He raised his eyes immediately and grinned with the cooperating half of his face. "Where have you been, son? I've been waiting."

The nurse gave Larry a quick nod, and left the room.

"At the clinic. I stayed overnight. As Sue told you, Fiona is a lot better. She may, really, become your little girl again."

"I'd like to live long enough for her to know me."

Larry sat in the chair the nurse had vacated.

Patrick stroked the Bible's silky pages, fingering the gold-rimmed edges. "I remember handing you my Bible when you were so young, five I think. And you could read then. I was amazed. Do you remember?"

"Of course. You were the first person, after I lost my family, who truly cared for me. I've thought about you every day of my life."

"But not always with admiration; not when you thought I'd abandoned you."

"I lost faith in you for a while, but I was very young."

A silence hung over them for a few moments. Patrick coughed lightly, his next few breaths coming

The Filigree Cross

shakily, and Larry was reminded of the short amount of time they might have together. "Patrick," he began.

"Yes, son?"

"Do you think our getting Fiona back is a miracle?"

Patrick was slow to answer. The old man's eyes were shaded by drooping lids. Larry couldn't read them. "No. I always felt she would return to us. Didn't you?"

"No," Larry confessed. "I'd begun to feel it was truly hopeless."

"Then you think it was a miracle?"

"For me it seems like repayment, for my giving up the ministry."

"And why did God want you to give it up?"

Larry didn't want to hurt Patrick, especially now, but he desperately needed some answers.

"Because I'm a fake, and He knows it." Larry held his breath. Would Patrick be shocked? Would it wound him?

But Patrick merely looked down to his Bible for a moment, then back to Larry. "What makes you a fake? You believe there is a God, I know you do."

"But I know it in some cerebral sense. I know it because I know people like you. I know it because of all the goodness in the world, despite man's natural inclination toward selfishness." He paused for a moment, then put his hand over his heart. "But I don't know it in here, in my heart. I don't feel any warmth, any personal security. I've never had a calling—"

"Our Lord doesn't need to beckon those who already hear."

Larry pleaded, "But I don't hear. I never did."

"Then who gave you your gift? Who gave you the ability to lead people to Him?"

"Patrick, I'm a natural-born hawker. I could probably make a million dollars selling can openers at a county fair."

"Then why didn't God put you in that kind of tent?"

Larry blinked back tears of frustration. Everything was so clear to Patrick and so muddy to him.

Patrick made a great effort to raise his head from the pillow and command Larry's attention. "Don't you see, son, how thoroughly and utterly you believe in God? You believe He's capable of punishing, then rewarding, you. You believe He's capable of bringing Fiona back to us. What you don't believe in, is yourself."

An overpowering sense of loneliness washed over Larry. He wanted to grab Patrick's shoulders and shake him, and beg, *but how do I come to believe in myself?*

Patrick sank deep into his pillow, eyes closed. He held up his hand, and Larry took it. Patrick whispered, "Our church has reached millions and millions of people all over the world because of you. I had the message and you had the voice."

He squeezed Larry's hand with the strength of a small child. "God knows what He's up to. Trust in Him."

The Filigree Cross

CHAPTER TWENTY-THREE

ON A SUNNY NOVEMBER AFTERNOON Larry sat with Fiona in the solarium at the back of the mansion. Outside, sun sparkled on determined clumps of snow in the otherwise brown lawn. Fiona had spent almost a month with Dr. Freidman, and now he turned her over to the family every afternoon, when, with their stories, they rebuilt the life she missed.

Fiona leaned forward, her tea cup balanced on her knee. "How did we survive?" she asked. "That early congregation was poor. And what about all the medical bills?"

"It was really hard for your folks to make the decision, but finally they used your college money," Larry answered. By mentioning the medical bills she had broached the subject of her attack, and he watched for a reaction.

Her eyes clouded and her gaze drifted inward. Was she remembering what she had suffered? Or the day she drove away with such high expectations? Then she pulled herself back. "How long did the church stay in that little building?"

"When that two-year lease was up, we moved to a slightly better part of town. Gillian didn't have to worry so much about the congregation being out on the street at night after prayer meetings."

"Was Mom working part time, like she always did when we stopped for the winter?"

"She worked at a pre-school, and also kept everything behind the scenes running smoothly for your dad. And, of course, raised Sue. At those prayer meetings Sue would either be asleep in the portable crib or bouncing on Gillian's lap." Larry didn't mention how often Gillian ran herself ragged, her beauty erased by weary eyes and slumping shoulders.

"I remember that Mom could always work wonders. Didn't Dad used to say that?"

"Every chance he got."

Fiona sat back. "I remember you at twenty-six. I wouldn't have guessed you were preacher material. Cowboy hats and tennis shoes and a bad attitude, as I recall."

Larry grinned, embarrassed. "I know, it's hard to believe. But the words came easily. Partly it was from spending so much time listening to Patrick, but it was more than that. Once I got started I could hardly control the thoughts that would pile up in my brain."

"I wish Dad were not so frail," Fiona said. "Wouldn't it be wonderful for the three of us to wander back over those roads we traveled?"

Larry couldn't think of anything better. "Be thankful you're recovering in time for him to see you well. He wanted that very badly."

"If not for that fight you were having with . . ."

"Mark McLaren."

The Filigree Cross

"If not for that, it mightn't have happened in time."

"And that's why I didn't sack the man outright, or worse."

"What were you fighting about?"

"McLaren and I disagree on a lot of things. This one just went a little too far. Since he seems truly remorseful, I've decided to let him stay on; it may not be for that long anyway." Larry didn't want to dwell on the fact that Patrick's death would mean the demise of the church. "Do you remember when you and I went to the camp meeting to see that faith healer?"

"That was fun."

"I kept counting the money he was pulling in and trying to figure out which ideas we could steal."

Fiona put her tea aside and leaned back into her chair.

"I'm sorry, I've tired you out," Larry said.

"It's pretty intense, trying to grasp all I have missed."

UPSTAIRS, SUE PACED HER BEDROOM. Jimmy was leaving for Hawaii in two weeks—he'd promised the church there. They had talked about marriage, and he was putting pressure on her to join him. Sue knew she would not be able to leave now with her grandfather so ill. However, it was unlikely he would live several more months. If she asked him, Jimmy would wait a reasonable time; the question then would be, could she leave her new-found mother?

She heard the door from the solarium open. Larry and Fiona must have finished with this day's reminiscences. It sometimes hurt Sue to see them together, always animated. Sue longed to be Fiona's daughter—loved unreservedly, sheltered and safe. But she and her mother were more like sisters. As a result, their talks were stilted, both of them groping to capture that lost relationship.

When Larry and Fiona were near the foot of the stairs, Sue called down to them. "Enough for today?"

Fiona answered, her voice sad. "I guess I'll never catch up."

Sue descended the stairs and hugged her mother. "Mom, if you're up to it, I'd like us to go for a short car ride. I need to talk to you."

Fiona turned to Larry. "Getting outdoors sounds like a good idea. We'll see you for dinner."

MOTHER AND DAUGHTER DROVE through the park, the lowering winter sunlight warm on their faces. They moved past thick tree trunks that broke the light into shafts. Sue felt those quick bursts of sun ticking off their time together, and realized that she had made up her mind about going with Jimmy.

"What were you two talking about today?" she asked.

"We had gone back to the early days. I was trying to get a sense of how Larry's role evolved from handyman to star."

"The local radio ministry invited Larry to be a guest speaker. I was only about five or six then, but Grandma told me about it years later. At first Larry refused; he felt that Grandpa should be the one to do the guest spot. But Grandpa and Grandma knew what was happening. Larry was the magnet that drew our audience. And still is. I'll show you some tapes of our services one day. You'll see what I mean."

The Filigree Cross

"I'd like to see the tapes," Fiona said, "but I have no trouble imagining it. I knew him as a run-down misfit, and even then he had a roguish charm." She thought of Larry studying the faith-healer. "I bet he's bold on stage. Does he strut and fling his arms?"

"Sort of," Sue answered. "It's not as obvious as that, but he certainly takes control of the stage, and everything else. Or used to." She pulled into a parking spot that allowed them a view of a foot bridge arching over a pond. Sue rolled her window down a couple of inches. Sharp air drifted across her face and she breathed deeply. She might miss this even while enjoying Hawaii's softness.

She turned toward her mother, reminded again that she had not inherited the bright eyes and russet hair.

"And now, with Dad's condition, the church is disbanded?" her mother asked.

"For the sake of our employees and the charities which the church supports, we thought about enlisting another minister. But we could think of no one to replace either Grandpa or Larry. It just wouldn't be *our* church anymore."

"What will you do now, Sue?"

Sue didn't answer immediately, so Fiona continued. "Why not go to Hawaii with Jimmy?"

Sue felt herself flush. "How did you know about that?"

"Larry, of course. He talks about you a lot."

"Really?"

"Yes. He thinks the world of you, Sue. He's always saying how much the ministry depended on your talents. You are so young to have been carrying all that responsibility, so why not go to Hawaii now? I hope you wouldn't stay here because of me."

"I have been worried about that."

"Don't be. As soon as the doctor releases me, I'm going to move into the house. I would love to care for Dad. And I could visit you. Airplanes make the trip across the Pacific regularly, though I'm a little apprehensive about experiencing that."

Sue took her mother's hand. "I keep forgetting all that you have to deal with."

"Don't feel sorry for me. It's exciting, actually. Like being a little kid, a new wonder every few minutes." Sue recognized false bravado in the words. As Fiona looked deep into the park, Sue saw her cheeks fall as though she was experiencing a sadness. Fiona's voice went soft. "I became childlike, because when you're a child you know someone is always looking after you. I didn't want to grow up."

She turned back to Sue, attempting a smile. "But we're getting off track. We were talking about you."

"I love Jimmy very much," she said.

"Then go. Call him as soon as we get back to the house. Do you know how precious each day is?"

BACK AT THE HOUSE, FIONA went to see Patrick. She was exhausted, but wanted to see him before she left. He lay perfectly still in the lamplight. Fiona kissed him on the forehead and his eyes snapped open. Recognition took a moment, then he gave her his half smile and reached for her hand.

Fiona perched on the wide bed. "Hi, Dad," she said.

"Hi, my little girl." He forced every syllable.

The Filigree Cross

"Do you need anything? Can I get you some water?"

The slow but firm shake of his head told her nothing was needed. "Just to see you is all," he muttered. He tried to press her fingers.

"We missed a lot of time together," Fiona began. "I'm so sorry about that."

"You were always in our hearts." He took a deep breath and closed his eyes as he let it out.

"Don't talk. Just rest." Fiona continued quickly so he wouldn't try to say anything further. "I remember all the wonderful times we had, you and Mom and me. Did you know how important I felt when, as such a young girl, I took the stage with you? The people adored you. I could see it in their eyes as they gazed upward, and I was so proud to be at your side. No one had a better childhood."

"Hard work," Patrick muttered, eyes still closed.

"Yes, it was. But it didn't hurt me, or Mom."

Patrick's face contorted into a grimace and tears formed at the edges of his eyes. Fiona dabbed at them with a tissue. "She was the best wife and mother in the world," she said.

Patrick took a shuddering breath. "Soon." The yearning tone in that single word told everything.

Fiona's throat constricted. Yes, soon, they would be together—and she would be alone again.

Patrick read her mind. "Larry's here," he whispered.

"Yes, Dad." She patted his hand. "Yes, Larry will be here. You don't have to worry about me."

Her voice threatened to break, so she stopped talking. Patrick took a deep breath and a small snore escaped him. But *would* Larry always be here for her? And on what terms? The church, which had become both his home and family, no longer existed. Larry's love for Patrick and Gillian kept him close now, but what would hold him after Patrick died? Didn't Larry have dreams of his own? Maybe this was his chance to escape his obligations to the Brannigan family. Did she want to become the next one of them to claim his time and energy? Maybe he would stay for her out of loyalty to her folks. That would be torment.

Fiona released Patrick's hand, watching for any indication that the movement disturbed him. When he didn't respond she moved to the window.

Barren tree branches stretched in black silhouette against the anemic sunset. She looked toward Larry's house. With the foliage gone, she could see a corner of his roof. Picturing him there, she wanted to imagine him bent over his desk, lost in concentration. But, instead, she could only see his long legs stretching out before him and his hands lying on the desk top. Along with her slow return to maturity had come a growing desire. Every movement of Larry's dragged her thoughts to the body beneath the elegant clothes. She wondered what his skin looked like, how the hair on his arms felt. His every gesture caused her breath to catch. And the discipline of keeping her feelings hidden added to the distance between them. Now, she gave in to it—felt his arms around her. The illusion was so strong she closed her eyes and gave herself over to the surge of warmth and longing that engulfed her. When she finally opened her eyes she was dizzy with the effort of tearing herself away.

The Filigree Cross

No, she wouldn't be able to stand his being so near. If he had no plans to move on, she would have to.

After asking the nurse to watch over Patrick, she walked to Larry's house.

WHEN THE DOORBELL RANG Larry realized he had been holding a carved grouse, its body and legs thick with finely chiseled feathers. His birds had become a comfort; he found that handling them, sometimes rubbing their backs, soothed him.

He was delighted to see Fiona, but she didn't even give him a chance to welcome her.

"Could you drive me back to the clinic now?" she asked.

"But, we were going to have dinner. Where's Sue?" He took her arm and pulled her inside, closing the door.

"Sue's probably with Jimmy. They'll be celebrating. She has decided to go to Hawaii with him."

"Really? That's great. Then let's you and I—"

As she looked up at him, he saw a rawness in her eyes that stopped his voice. He thought, crazily, that it was desire. But instantly it was gone, replaced by something flat. She put her hand to her throat as the color drained from her cheeks.

"What's the matter? Were you visiting with Patrick?"

"Yes. I guess that has got me down. I'm really tired. I'd like to get back and go to bed early."

"Of course."

IN THE CAR Fiona told Larry about her conversation with Sue and her decision to move into the mansion to be with Patrick.

"He'll be thrilled," Larry said, thinking how wonderful it would be to have her living just across the garden. But would he be able to keep her there after Patrick left them?

Fiona dashed those daydreams with her next statement. "You know, eventually, I'll bet Sue and Jimmy would invite me to Hawaii if I hinted. What do you think it would be like, living in paradise?"

Meanness, born of disappointment, colored his voice. "Oh, it probably wouldn't be what you envision."

"Surely they still have sunshine and beaches?" she teased.

"And a million tourists and traffic and cheap merchandise."

"Even on the Big Island?"

"Well, honestly, that may be a different story," he said. "I haven't been there for probably twenty years."

"Twenty years . . . how wonderful to look back and remember twenty years of life."

Larry's teeth clenched, too late to bite back all his stupid words. Fear of losing her was making him cruel. He reached out, took her hand from her lap and squeezed it. "I'm sorry. I'm just jealous. It will no doubt be wonderful."

The Filigree Cross

CHAPTER TWENTY-FOUR

LARRY DROVE TOWARD the administration offices of the church with a growing sense of loss. He had given up preaching, the core of his life, and with that went the flesh around it—the people he'd known and places he'd occupied for so long. As he parked the car and walked to the front entrance, Larry looked, perhaps for the last time, at the graceful building. When he and Patrick had decided to base the television ministry in Chicago, they visited dozens of possible properties. After an exhaustive search they'd been delighted to find this well-preserved structure. It had once been a private school in the countryside. Now, condominium buildings and professional offices encircled its wooded grounds.

He had come, today, to visit Technicolor and learn the details of the donation Johnny Cameron said had not been returned to his grandmother. It was only twenty dollars, a sum easily misplaced among their millions; that alone, would not be a concern. But the subsequent events involving the Camerons nagged at Larry. There had to be more to the story.

Marlene Baird

Technicolor rated high among the people Larry would miss. Tech had been a faithful and loyal employee, and his flamboyance was not like the act that Larry put on when performing. Tech's exuberance was real. Larry hated having to confront him about a possible money scam and hoped there was a good explanation.

A thick runner absorbed the sound of his footsteps. He fingered the textured wallpaper as he moved down the hallway. In shades of green with a swirling leaf design, it created a living background for the fabulous art collection. Italian and French madonnas hung near pastoral scenes. Portraits of historical religious figures shared the company of wildlife. Larry looked at everything anew.

As he approached Tech's office, Theresa stepped into the hallway, closing the door behind her. As soon as she saw him she cocked her head to the side and gave him a smile. She wore a full-length white fur coat. Larry thought it a fake, but that did nothing to detract from its effect. Walking toward him, she casually parted the front with gloved hands, revealing a red woolen dress underneath. A heavy pendant hung between her breasts. Her eyes sparkled.

"Larry, what a terrific surprise!" She walked right up to him, forcing him to stop. "We never see you anymore," she said, touching the lapel of his coat. Larry took her hand from his chest, then didn't know what to do with it.

He saw that his rebuff shook her composure.

"Sometimes I think you don't like me, even a little."

"Theresa—"

The Filigree Cross

She brought his hand to her lips and kissed his knuckles. He felt the warmth of her tongue. "Some day I'll change your mind."

She pulled her coat protectively around her and moved past him down the hallway.

LARRY KNOCKED ON TECH'S DOOR, waited a second, and entered. Tech rose from his chair and extended his hand across the desk. "I'm glad to see you, Larry. Wish you'd come over more often." Sitting back down, he hooked thumbs through his suspenders. "Now, what was it that sounded so serious on the phone?"

Larry sat opposite him. He looked around the office. Everyone else in the ministry enjoyed elegant bookshelves, walnut file cabinets, expensive desk accessories. Everything in Tech's office was functional. Steel file drawers, his jacket flung carelessly on a coat rack. Larry knew his closet was jammed with computer manuals, thick volumes of federal regulations, and unread newspapers. The desk was littered with files, pencils, overflowing ashtrays. If there was a money scam going on, he could certainly not judge Tech's motives by his surroundings.

"Looks as if you've hardly slowed down," Larry said.

Tech groaned. "The government never sleeps."

The silence, as they measured each other, was heavy with thoughts being arranged.

Larry began. "That Minneapolis trip . . . did you hear about a woman and her grandson who were invited to sit in the first row?"

Marlene Baird

Tech snapped his suspenders and sat up, elbows on the desk. "Sure. I remember them. Theresa brought me the kid's letter. His grandmother had sent a bunch of money, too much for the kid's liking, and he wanted it back. We sent it right away."

"Then you decided to invite them to the service?" The lack of a reasonable connection between these two actions was clear.

"Uh, yeah. Well, actually Theresa suggested it, and I agreed with her. The kid had said how much the grandmother loved you, etcetera." Tech waved his hands. "You know, on and on. Anyway, we thought it would be a nice gesture."

"The kid's name is Johnny Cameron, and he worked for us until he was laid off."

Tech's eyebrows rose. "He did? I must have seen the name, but it didn't connect."

"He and I were talking, and he mentioned that his grandmother had sent a small contribution to the church after Gillian's death."

Tech nodded. He dropped his gaze and absently rearranged a pile of papers on his desk. Then he rose and paced behind his desk, his back to Larry. The light from the window behind Tech silhouetted his dark form, swallowing the parrot colors. "It must have been a small amount. I don't remember exactly," he said.

"Twenty dollars."

Tech nodded. He lit a cigarette and took a deep draw, blowing the smoke upward. Then he turned to face Larry.

"There's no harm done."

"What does that mean?"

The Filigree Cross

"Do you remember when you were so adamant about sending back any money we received on Gillian's behalf?"

"Of course."

"Well, I thought that perhaps it was a poor decision, made at a bad time. You know, you and Patrick were hurting so much—"

"Get off it, Tech."

Tech stubbed his cigarette vigorously and ground it into the heavy glass ashtray.

He spoke quickly. "I siphoned off some of the smaller checks for a while. Set up a separate account. There's three hundred and thirty thousand dollars in it."

Tech dropped into his chair. He ran his tongue back and forth under his top lip.

"Every original penny is still in the account?" Larry asked.

Tech nodded.

"When were you going to do something with it? When the ministry closed down for good?"

"I honestly don't know." Tech began to wave his arms in the air. "Maybe never. Larry, you know the actual money means nothing to me. Dollars are simply numbers. It was a game. See what *could* be done. There's so damn much money involved here that it loses its meaning."

Larry held up his hand to stop the flow of words.

"You've been invaluable to Patrick," he said. "This is hard to believe."

Tech had the decency not to explain further.

"How long have you been with us? About fifteen years?"

"Fourteen and a little."

"Can I ask you something very personal?"

"Sure."

"What is your relationship with Theresa?"

Tech's head snapped back. "Theresa? Why do you care?"

"It's important," Larry said.

"I think a lot of her. She just puts up with me."

"Do you think she could put up with you on a long-term basis?"

Tech sighed. "I don't know. Sometimes I think she's in love with someone else. But she sticks around; I can't figure it out."

Larry stood and picked up his coat. Tech jumped to his feet.

Larry said, "Let's call the three hundred and thirty thousand severance pay, with a condition."

Tech moved around the desk, arms extended. "Hell, Larry. I don't want it."

Larry opened the door. "Theresa's a nice woman. She deserves a long, sunny holiday. Take her far away," he said as he closed the door behind him.

The Filigree Cross

CHAPTER TWENTY-FIVE

PATRICK DIED ON A BLEAK DAY at the end of November. Freezing wind alternately sighed, then shrieked around the corners of the mansion as though wailing his passing. Television stations and newspapers carried the story of his demise, and that of the church, dashing the hopes of millions of people who prayed daily for the resurrection of the Church of God's Love.

MAUREEN CAMERON DROPPED the paper and sat back in her chair, tears streaming down her cheeks. She had prayed hard for Larry Broadfellow's return, sometimes for intervals so long that her mind became blurred. And now it seemed an impossibility. Hundreds of times she had replayed the night the church service came to Minneapolis—Larry Broadfellow speaking directly to her, then seeming to give Johnny a purpose for his life. How could something so special end like this?

Johnny had been laid off by the church when Rev. Brannigan became too ill to preach, and, since coming home, his disappointment had grown into despondency. He spent long hours in his room, then emerged with a practiced nonchalance, rendered a lie by red-ringed eyes and piles of used tissues in his wastebasket.

She'd plead, "Tell me what you're struggling with, Johnny. You can tell me." But he couldn't. The burden on his young shoulders seemed to be heavier than she, herself, had ever been, and for some reason it was his alone.

She knew all the signs of a life going haywire; Johnny's mom had taught her that. The lesson had come too late the first time; she could not let it happen again.

She wheeled into the kitchen and pulled paper and pen from the shallow cupboard drawer. She'd just begun her letter when she heard Johnny's truck. Quickly, she tucked the paper and pen between her thigh and the wheelchair.

JOHNNY REMOVED HIS SHOES and entered as quietly as possible. As he moved on stockinged feet past the kitchen doorway, his grandmother's voice stopped him.

"Were you out all night?"

Johnny jerked to a stop in the hall.

"Uh," was all he could manage. He'd had no practice lying to his grandmother and a fierce headache dulled his thinking. He backed up and entered the kitchen.

"Gram, you've been crying," he said.

"Reverend Brannigan died," she whispered, reaching for her tissue.

The Filigree Cross

Johnny sank to his knees and put his arm around her shoulder. "Oh, Gram," he said.

Suddenly aware of the liquor on his breath, he rose again, but was surprised to feel a tug in his own breast. He had never even spoken to Reverend Brannigan, but he thought of Sue and Billy Sills and all the people at the ministry who truly loved the man. Even Larry Broadfellow might actually be suffering. He wanted to feel good about Broadfellow suffering—it would make his own turmoil more bearable. The only person in the world to whom he'd confessed his crisis had ignored him, treated him like a child, and sent him on his way.

He touched his grandmother's shoulder. "This is the end of the church then," he said quietly. "Gram, I wish there was something I could do to help because it's meant so much to you."

"And you, too," she said, searching his face.

"Once."

Maureen took his hand. "Johnny, please, you must tell me what has made you so unhappy. I just can't believe that Larry Broadfellow didn't want to help you."

Johnny slumped into a chair beside her. "Well, Gram, he didn't. I hate to tell you, but he was standoffish and too busy for me and only told me what a tough road it would be, and that he'd done everything wrong and I shouldn't try to be like him."

His grandmother gasped.

"You wanted to hear, Gram."

"But did you tell him? I mean really explain to him how you felt?"

"I wanted to, but he wasn't paying that much attention." He stood up, pushing hair back from his

Marlene Baird

face. "I'm done with it Gram. I've got new friends now."

"Are they friends, or are they just handy to party with?"

He started to leave the room but the intensity in her voice stopped him. "Johnny, wait. So Larry Broadfellow didn't meet your expectations—"

"Gram, millions and millions of people believed him and he fooled them all." Johnny had to control himself to keep from shouting at her. "He only proved that I was right not trusting him in the first place. How can you still defend him?"

Her jaw dropped and all animation left her face. She seemed to be looking far into the future. Johnny noticed for the first time the fragile folds of skin that drooped like umbrellas over the outside edges of her eyes. "I'll never give up." she said. "Larry Broadfellow brought me so much happiness, so much hope. I'll never be able to think his words were not true."

Johnny left the room, unable to console her and unwilling to bend. He fell on his bed and immediately was lost in disjointed sleep. He grappled, again, with a voice that would not be silenced. Confused, he sweated and twisted in his bed, the sheets binding his legs.

CHAPTER TWENTY-SIX

LARRY FROWNED AT THE RINGING phone, put aside the wood carving and picked up the receiver with a dusty hand. Mark asked how Sue and he were coping. Larry said they were managing. That was putting a good face on it. His voice was cold; he didn't care if Mark knew he was unhappy about being disturbed.

"Larry, you can't imagine the amount of mail down here. We don't have near enough staff to deal with it."

"Deal with it?" Larry asked. "Surely people don't actually expect replies."

"Not generally," Mark said. "But many people are truly torn up. It's as if they've lost a loved one, a member of their own family. I really think we need to draft a letter. A few kind words."

"Saying what?"

"They don't want to believe that, beyond losing Patrick, they've lost the entire church. They want you back more than ever."

Larry sighed. Would it never go away?

"I'd really appreciate it if you'd take a look at some of these for yourself," Mark urged.

"After the funeral's out of the way," Larry snapped, and hung up.

He picked up the largest of the pieces of wood before him. Every moment since Patrick's death, when he wasn't needed elsewhere, he had been ensconced in his workshop. Work table, bench, lamps, the high bridge of his nose, everything, was covered by a layer of powder-fine dust. Closing his eyes, he ran his fingers along the surface of the wood, felt a minute change in grain direction, and picked up a piece of sandpaper as fine as linen writing paper. He stroked in a long, straight motion, until he could no longer feel any blemish. He checked and rechecked every surface of this gift to Patrick. Finally satisfied, he took a shaving brush and dusted each piece. They were ready for paint. The first coat would dry by evening, the second overnight. Then he would assemble the pieces and take the work to the artist he'd located who would add the fine script.

FOR THREE DAYS LARRY HAD watched thousands of Patrick's followers stream past his casket. There seemed to be no end to the love for this man. Now, as the memorial service began, the open casket stretched before them, bearing the repository of their love. Larry sat with Fiona on his left and Sue on his right, each of them clutching his hand. He felt the press of Sue's new engagement ring against his flesh. Jimmy sat on her other side, his arm draped across her shoulders.

The pews behind them were not full. It had been necessary to limit the number of people allowed at the service, so it was decided to include only close friends

The Filigree Cross

and church employees. This served Larry, who felt ill-equipped to present the eulogy.

Occasionally people rose and passed the casket. Larry had said dozens of goodbyes, and had one farewell left. He wanted to be the last one to approach Patrick.

A few minutes after the appointed starting time, in the alcove to their right, Larry saw Rev. Alfred Pierce adjusting his robes. The organ music swelled, and he knew the service would begin immediately. Dropping the women's hands, he quickly unwrapped the small parcel he had been holding on his lap and went forward.

He leaned over Patrick's body, trying for the last time to draw strength from the man who had shaped his life. But Patrick's countenance was far too calm for this earth. He seemed finished with them, gone to a better place, leaving them to earn their way.

Larry placed the carving in the crook of Patrick's arm. It was a small sailing ship with a lustrous black hull, gleaming masts, and crisp sails. The delicate white script on its prow read, "Gillian."

Then he reached up and closed the casket.

REVEREND PIERCE DESCRIBED Patrick's life of devotion, citing the millions of people who had come to Christ through his tent-to-television ministries. He recounted Patrick's love of family, his steadfastness through private crises, his unwavering trust in the Lord. Larry mentally urged the pastor on, hoping he would cover everything so there would be little left for Larry to say.

Fiona leaned slightly into him. He turned to see tear-filled eyes and a mouth drawn down. He tilted his head so she could whisper in his ear, "Please say thank-you for me. I never did it properly. Thank him for caring for Sue."

Too soon it was time. He stood on shaky legs and moved behind the podium. Gripping its edges, he kept his eyes high, away from the coffin and away from the family.

"I know we can all echo everything Reverend Pierce has said," he began. "Most of you here today knew Patrick personally and can corroborate from your own experience his unending patience and kindness."

Larry's mind searched for words. Every phrase seemed inadequate, for Patrick deserved the highest possible tribute. While he subconsciously worked that out, he complied with Fiona's request.

"Patrick's daughter, Fiona, has asked me to make a tribute on her behalf. As some of you know, for most of her life, Fiona has been unable to care for her daughter, Sue. Patrick and Gillian raised Sue. They prayed constantly that Fiona would come back into their lives, even though it meant she would reclaim her child whom they loved as their own. Gillian didn't live to see her prayers answered, but they were. Through God's blessing, Fiona is with us today to offer Gillian and Patrick her thanks."

Larry felt his shoulders relax. His fingers loosened their grip on the lectern. His legs held him firmly. He had said, 'through God's blessing,' and found that he meant it. The essence of the words struck home for the first time. He had not the slightest doubt that he spoke the truth. God didn't send Fiona back to him as a

The Filigree Cross

reward for not preaching. How foolish, how selfish, of him to even think such a thing. And God didn't give Fiona back to Patrick and Gillian, good as they were—for surely He would have done it when they were well and able to enjoy their gift. Fiona's return to the world was simply a blessing. All the parts of her life—the happy youth, the pain, the long confinement, the victory—had given those around her joy or testing. And that is what we all are to one another, Larry thought, imperfect partners, offering to one another every conceivable turn of events, forcing us to continue to learn and to grow.

There seemed to be absolution for himself in these thoughts, as though his own false life had some merit. He moved out from behind the altar and stood, hands at his sides. His eyes met Fiona's, and then Sue's.

"I love God for what he has done," he said simply. "I love the God who brought Fiona back, and the God who took Patrick. Everything in its time, His perfect time.

"We had Patrick among us for eighty years. More than fifty of those years were spent spreading the word. But even the Savior's messengers, perhaps especially them, bear injustices, have periods of deep despair. Since Patrick met everything in life with faith, nothing could defeat him."

Larry felt his own sense of defeat lifting. His eyes fell to where Patrick lay just before him. They'd had a few short conversations in the last days, but Patrick had been far too weak to be burdened with deep questions. Larry had always meant to ask Patrick what his wishes were after he was gone. He had waited too long, and lost the opportunity. If he could do just one thing for Patrick, what would it be? What could he do that would properly honor the man to whom he owed his very existence? His eyes ranged over the audience. They sat, unearthly quiet, waiting for his next words.

He spoke as if they'd been privy to his thoughts. "I think Patrick would want, above all, to have the church live on."

He heard one sharp intake of breath and general mumbling among those gathered.

"But we can't sustain a church on sand. Patrick was our rock; how do we proceed without him?"

Just as they had done when he was on stage, unbeckoned words skittered into his consciousness. They lined themselves up into sentences, as clear as if they had been painstakingly crafted and displayed on a teleprompter. This is what Patrick must have meant about the Holy Spirit working in our lives. Larry realized the import of the words and was frightened. If he made this promise, and failed, he would fall into a despair deeper than that which he had already experienced; he would bring even more pain to Sue and how many others whose lives were bound to the ministry. But he had no time to ponder—the teleprompter in his mind was moving on, he was falling behind. He spoke quickly to catch up, knowing he promised blindly, was responding only to some command to become a better man.

"No one can replace Patrick, but I will become the best imitation that I'm capable of. I'm going to enter the ministry properly, through study and devotion. I know I will be severely tested, and, if I meet those challenges, that will be my tribute to Patrick: to bring his church back."

The Filigree Cross

Larry bowed his head to still the buzzing that crept along the pews. As silence was restored, he began a prayer. "Dear Lord, we feel You here with us now as we say farewell to Your good steward." The words flowed, smooth and strong. As their meaning became more clear to him than it ever had before, he began to comprehend the awesome power of preaching. He was shaken to realize that for the first time his words were not hollow, not shiny bubbles to be lightly tossed for entertainment, but heavy things, landing densely in people's hearts. And their rhythm derived, not from the cadence of prancing showmanship, but from the beating of his own heart, his submission to God's will.

CHAPTER TWENTY-SEVEN

THE EUPHORIA DID NOT LAST. Before the limousine arrived at the cemetery Larry was swimming in doubts. The enormity of his public declaration assaulted him. How could he ever hope to be the true Christian that Patrick was, or even become a fully ordained minister? His formal education had stopped at high school. While he was speaking to the assembled mourners everything had seemed possible. His words had taken on substance, had become so much more than an accumulation of syllables. He recalled feeling the weighty significance of them, perhaps understanding them for the very first time. Had God given him that glimpse of glory to hang on to during his arduous test ahead? If so, he would have to cling to the memory of that moment, allow himself to re-live it and re-live it, because, so soon, his confidence was eroding.

As the service came to a close, Larry fought the final goodbye. He was losing his mentor, his friend, and the only father he could remember. To the end, Patrick had told Larry to trust in God's plan, not to

The Filigree Cross

question His methods. How he wished to sit at Patrick's bedside again and be reassured.

"Stay with me, Patrick," he begged, as the body was lowered into the ground.

LARRY BEGAN A ROUTINE OF HOURLY prayers. However, talking to God, without an audience whose reaction he could sense, left him with no way to measure his effectiveness. Sometimes it felt as if he were talking to his own heart. Did answers come from his subconscious—a result of his exposure to so many years of Patrick's preaching? For he knew, intellectually, the proper responses. How did one come to trust one's inner voice?

He was a master of words and now they were turning on him. He had interpreted the Lord's messages so often that words like redemption and sacrifice and forgiveness were too familiar. He waited for God's answers, but they sounded too much like what he had been spewing for years. He couldn't discern the difference between God's voice and the echo of his own memory. Something was missing, some connection, and it frightened him to think that, without Patrick's guidance, he would be unable to find it.

ON THE MORNING of Sue and Jimmy's departure for Hawaii, Larry had risen early and spent hours sorting through such jumbled, circular thoughts. When the doorbell rang he was grateful for the distraction. He ran his hands through his hair and glanced in the mirror over the mantle, enjoying these simple, human, responses to a summons.

Fiona stood framed in the doorway, her hair floating free, her face buffed to a shine by the crisp air. A bulky sweater enveloped her small frame. Her freshness buoyed his own spirits, and he felt a surge of vitality.

"Sue and Jimmy are almost ready to leave. I know you want to see them off."

He took her arm and they walked through the dormant garden. They saw Sue and Jimmy embrace on the steps of the mansion, as a limo driver loaded their bags.

Fiona's gaze lingered on her daughter.

"You'll miss her," Larry offered.

"Only until Christmas. I expect it to take me that long to pack up the folks' treasures and close up the house. Imagine, Christmas with palm trees." She tugged at his arm. "You'll be lonely. Why won't you come over, at least for the holidays?"

Her appeal seemed earnest and open, unlike the restraint he had recently felt in her presence. Larry wanted nothing more than to spend every day with her, whether in the islands or anywhere else, but Fiona needed lots of time. Time to learn about the world; maybe even time enough to fall in love with someone else.

"It sounds great, but I've committed to some volunteer work this year. I think I drew kitchen duty."

Sue walked toward them and took their hands. "I'll miss you both so much," she said.

"Be happy, sweetheart," Fiona said, hugging her.

"I'll be there in April for the wedding," Larry promised. He embraced Sue and kissed her cheek.

The Filigree Cross

"This is hard. It's like I'm having to give you away twice."

As the limo bore Sue and Jimmy away, Fiona wiped her eyes.

"Why not have dinner with me?" Larry asked. "It's just the two of us now, for a while."

Fiona hesitated, then said, "But let's go out. I saw a new seafood place advertised."

THE FOOD WAS EXCELLENT, the atmosphere adequate, but instead of relishing being with the person most important to him in the world, Larry felt distant from Fiona. He had spent an inordinate amount of time on his shower and choice of clothes whereas Fiona had on the same slacks and sweater she'd worn in the afternoon. When he took her arm to enter the restaurant, she seemed to tense at his touch. That stiffness did not leave her during the rest of the evening. Though separated by only a small table, it was as if she were already two thousand miles away, or wished she were. Without Sue or Patrick as a fulcrum, he and Fiona could find no balance.

As soon as they returned home, Fiona hurried into the mansion, leaving him standing at the door. Walking to his own home, Larry realized how much he'd been looking forward to having Fiona to himself for a few weeks, and how misguided those romantic notions had been.

THERE WAS A TELEPHONE MESSAGE from Mark, saying Larry could call him at home as late as ten o'clock.

Marlene Baird

"The mail is still piling up," Mark said. "We need to decide what to reply. Is there even a very remote chance you're going to resume the broadcasts within the next year?"

"I don't see how I can do it properly that soon with all the work that's ahead of me. We'll have to see if anyone remembers us a couple of years from now."

"Still, maybe we can draft up something to tell people we'll be back eventually."

"I'll come in tomorrow," Larry promised. "We can talk about it."

CANVAS BAGS OF UNOPENED MAIL cluttered his office, and with every letter he read Larry was reminded how these people counted on the revival of the church.

He dipped into a bag and picked up an envelope at random. It was addressed to him, marked 'Personal and Confidential' in fat, red letters. He could hardly believe his eyes when he saw the return address. Maureen Cameron. Larry recalled Johnny's visit to his house and how insensitive he had been to the young man because of his own turmoil. He shook his head, remembering with shame, his self-absorption. He read her letter twice, then picked up the phone.

JOHNNY SHOOK COBWEBS FROM HIS brain. He'd worked a long shift, slept hard, and stumbled into the kitchen to the ringing of the telephone.

"Johnny, this is Larry Broadfellow."

Johnny woke up quickly. "Reverend Broadfellow?" His mind spun. What had Gram been up to now?

The Filigree Cross

He heard the evangelist chuckle. "Soon you'll be able to call me that, and I won't even argue. But I wanted to know how you've been since you left Chicago."

"Oh, okay. Gram's doing pretty good." Did she insist that Broadfellow call him?

"Well, she told me you've been troubled. And I'd like to help."

Johnny wanted to sink through the floor.

"I also want to apologize for the short shift I gave you when you visited me. You were looking for guidance then, and I let you down terribly. I'm very sorry. Do you still think about entering the ministry?"

Johnny rubbed one bare foot on the other. He felt mortified. Gram must have *begged* Broadfellow to get this much of his attention. He considered lying.

"Please understand, son, that I know something of what you're going through. I've decided to become ordained myself, and at my age it's going to be a long haul."

Maureen wheeled into the room.

Johnny put his hand over the mouthpiece. "It's Reverend Broadfellow. I don't know what to say."

She reached for the phone. "If you won't talk to him, I will."

Johnny moved the receiver out of her range. "Okay."

He began slowly. "I think about it all the time, but I'm still not sure—"

"I think you'll always regret not having tried if you don't do it now. The church has a scholarship program and I carry a little weight with the directors. Full

Marlene Baird

college tuition and living expenses, plus a divinity school—whatever you need, to go as far as you want."

Once again Johnny put his hand over the mouthpiece. He told his grandmother about the offer. "It can't be for real, Gram."

She took the receiver from him. "Reverend Broadfellow?" she said. "He accepts."

CHAPTER TWENTY-EIGHT

FIONA HAD BEEN TURNED AWAY from him for most of the drive to the airport. As she spoke she continued to look over her right shoulder, addressing the window or the passing street. "I'm worried sick about flying. I wish you were coming along." Larry heard more anger in her voice than fear. This is what she had said she wanted, and now she seemed to blame him for her own decision.

Though he saw her touch the side of her face to wipe away a trailing tear, he couldn't tell her that he longed to go with her. "Aren't you happy about going to be with Sue?" he asked.

She stared straight out the windshield now, as if the rear bumpers of the cars ahead were fascinating. With no inflection in her voice, she replied, "I've been released from a nightmare that could easily have claimed my entire life. I've learned that I'm a mother to an intelligent and loving child. If nothing else good ever happens to me I'll be more grateful than I could ever express. But even all of that is not happiness."

After a few minutes, she twisted around in her seat, more in his direction, tucking one leg under the other.

She drew in a long breath. "I'm acting like a child. I'm sorry. Being with Sue and Jimmy will be delightful."

She rested a hand on his arm. He resisted the temptation to cover her hand with his own.

"You know, we're both starting over," she said. "With me it is obvious. But you've also been doing something you didn't truly understand for years. Was there ever a time when you actually decided that evangelism would be your life?"

"I simply took the easy road for the most part. Perhaps that was my mistake. If I'd taken a risk, stepped outside my comfort zone, maybe I'd have been able to see."

"See what?"

"That I was merely a showman," he said.

Fiona spoke slowly, choosing her words. "Sue probably understands your contribution more than anyone else, and she would not agree with that assessment. You have been so much more." She moved her hand to the back of his neck. Larry could not help leaning into her touch as her fingers lingered before dropping away. It almost caused him to miss the turnoff, and he swung across the solid line into the airport approach lane.

Fiona straightened in her seat and said, "You don't have to park. Just leave me at the curb."

But he did park—anything to prolong her presence. They checked in, then found the gate, just as early boarding had begun. Fiona fussed with her ticket envelope, then shoved it in a pocket and said, "I'd better get going." But she didn't step away.

He took both her hands; they were icy cold. He cleared his throat. "Fiona, be happy." She gripped his hands, staring up at him. Larry fumbled for words to replace what he really wanted to say. "I hate to let you go—"

"Then don't," she said. Her face drained of color. Her mouth opened slightly and her eyes seemed enormous.

"It's just like when you were eighteen and going off to college. You've got everything before you. You should have the chance to embrace it all, without ties."

"Larry, do you love me?"

His legs went weak, and for a moment the room swam around him. He stroked her arms. "You must know I do, that I always have."

"Then, please, don't send me away again."

She sank against him and he could feel her heartbeat. He hugged her close, kissing the top of her head. She could be his forever, if he held her one more minute. Before his resolve could melt, he murmured, "It's last call. You don't want to miss the flight."

She jerked away from him, her eyes flaring with anger and hurt. "How can you?"

"You'll be safe this time," Larry said. "I promise."

AN INTERMINABLE WEEK LATER, Larry ripped open Fiona's letter. If she asked him, again, he would go to her, for the past days had been as empty as any he'd ever known.

Dear Larry,

I hated you as I ran away, and only minutes later would have given anything to have you beside me. Terrified is not strong enough a word for what I felt as we lifted off. I think the arm rests on the seat they put me in must still bear indents from my fingers. It probably took an hour before I actually sank down into my seat, confident that the plane would hold us.

We lifted into blinding sun, the plane's tiny shadow flitting along on the clouds below. I felt as small as that speck of shade, so easily obliterated by passing gusts of mist.

I expect there are hundreds of such fears to be conquered, and I can see that it will be better to face them on my own. With each success will come confidence, and every time I'll think of you, and your great generosity.
Love, Fiona

The Filigree Cross

CHAPTER TWENTY-NINE

EYES BLEARY AND OUT OF FOCUS, Larry tossed his book aside and pushed up from the depths of the easy chair. The soft leather had not released the imprint of his body for three weeks. As he passed the ornate mirror over the mantel, he avoided his likeness. Rubbing at stubble on his chin he parted the drapes with one hand, and flinched at the light. All outdoors glittered white. Thick berms of drifted snow rolled away from the house, undulating around black tree trunks. Near the window, delicate, three-pronged tracks traced over a snow bank. Was a bird looking for its buried home?

Winter had lost patience with teasing. A crippling blizzard had forced all thinking Chicagoans indoors but Larry barely noticed; he seldom left his home. Again, his eyes strayed across the grounds, between spidery tree limbs, searching out the eaves of the mansion—that beautiful shell from which all precious life had fled.

Gloria's voice startled him. She and Simon still lived in the caretakers' quarters. She cooked for him

Marlene Baird

daily and cleaned around him a couple of times a week.

"One day I'll come and find you buried alive under all these books, or blinded from all the reading you do," she said, standing at the doorway of his den holding a package wrapped in tin foil. She put the bundle down and pulled off her coat and scarf.

She went to the kitchen and came back carrying a dinner plate. It held three-quarters of a dried pork chop and sticky apple sauce. "You hardly ate a thing last night, Larry. You're getting skinny. And look at you. It's past two o'clock and you're not even dressed. Have you slept?"

"A little. Don't worry about me."

"I know you'd never let yourself go like this if the Brannigans were here to see it." She picked up two dry-ringed coffee cups and returned, muttering, to the kitchen. He heard dishes clattering.

He shuffled back toward his chair, stepping over piles of reading materials. Most of the books he paged through day and night were not textbooks that would help him toward his divinity degree—he had found he could, easily, master the studies ahead of him. What challenged him, now, were the great works of philosophy—the kinds of books that kept the mind engaged long after the body succumbed. In that there were far more questions than answers, they paralleled his life.

But he had lost his direction. He tried every day, through introspection and prayer, to recapture the glowing spirit that had filled him during Patrick's memorial service. He ached to feel that glorious sureness which had given him the strength to promise

The Filigree Cross

to rebuild the church. But Fiona's leaving had increased his despair, contributed to further self-doubt. The entire family had moved on; he could no longer see his role in their lives, and, therefore, in their church.

Just as he sat down, the phone rang. He was tempted to ignore it; it would be Mark worrying over another threatened litigation. Canceled engagements had brought upon them the ire of contract attorneys around the world.

Larry answered just ahead of the machine.

"I need a few approvals," Mark began, and launched into a litany of woes from over-stocked suppliers, rental companies and a charter airline, all financially damaged by the church's hiatus.

"Try not to make too many enemies, Mark. We don't want to give our lawyers any more work than necessary."

"I can promise them future business, when we get back into operation," Mark said hopefully.

Larry had serious doubts that there would be any future business. "Go easy on that. Our timetable is uncertain."

Their conversation continued, Larry's attention waning. Absently, he picked up a small carving of a goose. It was crude, a very early one, done at the Madison orphanage when he was a teenager. His fingers grazed sharp edges. The head, disproportionally large, almost toppled the bird. Many times he had been tempted to perfect it, but had left it alone as a reminder of how far he'd come as a craftsman. Now, he identified with the deformed bird—awkward, unattractive, useless except as a comparison to better species.

After talking to Mark, Larry made an effort to gather the books scattered around the room.

"I'll do that," Gloria said, having apparently finished her other chores.

"No. It's my mess. You go on; I promise to do better tomorrow." He helped her into her coat, anxious to be alone again.

"I left you a salmon loaf. Just heat it up," she said.

Beginning the process of tidying the room, Larry lifted a heavy volume from the floor beside his chair and Gillian's damaged cross fell to the carpet. He often fingered it while reading. On difficult days it was a reminder of his own twisted life, but on better days, being Gillian's possession, it brought her closer to him. Rubbing the cross between thumb and finger, he might sit back and gaze at the opposite wall. The first memory was always that of holding her hand on the steps of the church orphanage; to a desperate five-year-old she was safety and warmth. When he was a slovenly drunk who stumbled upon their road ministry, she had challenged him to change his life. He had watched her sacrifice for her husband and daughter. How many times had he marveled at the power of her lovely voice rising above that of the congregation? Then, with her final letter, she had forced him to examine his life again. That was proving a horrendous task but, even as he struggled with that, he saw his former falseness for what it was and would not reclaim his fame, were it offered.

Larry stood in the middle of the room holding the cross, lost in such thoughts. For the first time he saw

The Filigree Cross

that Gillian's death had been the rolling pebble that foretells a landslide, and all his personal woes and those of the church had rolled over them when she left. Larry had always spoken of Patrick as the foundation of the church, but Gillian had been its core.

For all her exposure to faith, living with Patrick as an example, she had turned away from God. Larry knew that he was perilously close to giving up himself. At least one person would understand. He put the cross to his lips, set it gently in his desk drawer and slid it closed.

When the room looked organized again, he shaved and dressed properly for his dinner, then found he was not hungry. As darkness fell he pulled on a jacket and wandered outside. His breath frosted on the air; his footsteps echoed sharply on the recently cleared walkways. Circling the mansion, he recalled Fiona's early, hesitant visits with Patrick. All Larry had wanted then was for her to get well; all he wanted now was for her to need him. "Selfish," he muttered. How could he expect to experience love and comfort? He had not earned it, and saw no way to do so.

There had been a bottle of whiskey stashed in his closet since the day he announced he was leaving the church. Countless times he had imagined opening it and diving headlong into escape. Tonight it beckoned as never before. He had been more unhappy in the recent past, more lost, but tonight he seemed to have a clear, unemotional view of a very bleak future. He hurried back to his home and the release that was hidden there.

Marlene Baird

AN HOUR LATER THE DOORBELL RANG. Larry lurched from his slumped position at the kitchen table. He grabbed his glass, drained the last few drops and rinsed it. He stuck the bottle beneath the sink. Someone punched the doorbell several times in quick succession.

She stood in the spilling doorway light, stunningly beautiful, her dark hair piled high above dangling silver earrings.

"Thank goodness. I'm freezing." She jumped inside.

She wore high-heeled black sandals and a coat which fell open, revealing a tight red sweater beneath.

"Theresa," Larry said. "What—?"

Stepping up to him, she kissed him lightly on the lips. "Merry Christmas," she said, her breasts touching his chest. Musky perfume mingled with the crisp air as he closed the door. As she moved down the hallway ahead of him, she slipped out of the coat and her taut hips and thighs were perfectly outlined in black tights.

She paused between the kitchen and the den, unsure which room to enter.

He pointed to the kitchen, a defensive move. "I was about to make some coffee."

She pulled a chair away from the table and sat, crossing her long legs. Her ankles, pink from cold, were sharp-boned. As she moved her foot nervously, one sandal dangled, caught only by perfectly manicured toes. Larry had to pull his eyes away. His legs coursed with energy. Don't be a damn fool, he warned himself. You're just unhappy and vulnerable right now.

The Filigree Cross

"This is a surprise," he said, filling the carafe with water.

"Nothing for me," she said. "Well, nothing to drink." Foregoing the coffee, he sat opposite her. A queer thought came to him—she was the devil. Larry laughed inside. God had set him up, then sent him temptation in its purest form.

"You were smiling. That's a good sign," she said.

"Didn't you leave town some time ago? I mean, I thought—"

"You thought I was with Tech. He's found a good job in New York, but I don't like that city, it swallows me up. By the way, he didn't take that severance you offered him."

"Mark told me. That was decent of him. So, do you need work? I can make some calls."

Black lashes, resembling soft brushes, blinked at him. She leaned forward on her elbows. "Larry, please. I didn't come looking for a recommendation. I can't get you off my mind. If you're human, and that's always been questionable to me, you must be so alone. Is there anything I can do?"

She was no good at sincerity—no better than he was at denying his desire. A silly little black bag, too small to hold anything, sat between them. She scratched it with a fingernail the exact color of her sweater. Larry imagined its sharpness on his skin.

As if reading his thoughts, she moved around the table and stood close behind his chair. She didn't touch him, but he could feel the heat of her body and could smell her scent. Suddenly her lips were against his ear, her hands on his chest.

A low moan escaped his throat before he could stop it. He took hold of her exploring hands, stilling them. "Theresa, this isn't what you want."

She whispered, "I'm pretty sure I know what I want." Her breath caressed his cheek.

"Let's talk about what we both want," he offered.

She straightened and walked around the room. She tossed her head, fighting embarrassment. "Why can't I get close to you? Am I some kind of freak?"

"Sit down. You're making me dizzy wandering around like that."

She folded herself back into the chair.

"Theresa, you're a lovely woman. If I'm distant it's because you come on so strong. I feel on guard with you. Like right now. Showing up, unexpectedly."

"Well, pardon me for not waiting for an invitation," she snapped. "I thought I might die of old age first."

He rose, stood beside her chair and took her arm, pulling her to her feet. "Come on, time to go. Let's pretend this didn't happen."

She tried to twist away. "*You're* the pretender. I knew it. You just don't like women—"

His gripped tightened. "Theresa, stop. You'll regret this tomorrow."

"And you think you won't? And a hell of a lot more than you can imagine."

Angry, Larry yanked her arm. She fell against him and held herself close. Thighs, sharp hip bones, breasts, all pressed into his flesh. Perfume, mixed with her own sultry essence, clouded his resolve. Moist lips sought his, and her kiss sent him spiraling to depths of pleasure too long unmined.

The Filigree Cross

HOURS LATER HE ROLLED OUT OF bed. He was not hung-over; he hadn't had enough whiskey for that. He wished he had drunk more—enough to help excuse his behavior.

Theresa slept through his showering and dressing. She slept through his remorseful pacing of the den, the purposeful clatter of coffee-making. Finally, he prepared a tray with coffee and toast and took it to her. Still, she slumbered, content as a puppy. Larry reminded himself she was hardly that innocent but that did nothing to allay his guilt.

He slid the tray onto the bureau, knocking over a framed picture of Fiona taken the day of her final release from the clinic.

Theresa's voice teased. "Dressed already? What a shame."

She leaned back on her elbows, her exquisite torso exposed to the morning light. She patted the bed. "Come here."

Larry approached, searching for words. She took his hand and pulled him down for a kiss. His hesitancy brought a flash of anger, darkening her eyes. Her voice was low. "Don't do this, Larry. Don't do this to me."

"Theresa, I—"

Suddenly she was kneeling on the bed, pelting his chest with her fists. He reined in her arms and she collapsed backward. He expected tears, but she bristled, and spit out the words. "Do you know what you are? A selfish pig! And you're going to be so damn sorry. I could have saved you, you creep; now you can go to hell."

She jumped from the bed, grabbing at her clothes. Larry, wondering what she meant by "saving" him, turned away as she struggled into the black tights. Two minutes later she bolted through the doorway, yelling, "Believe me, you'll regret this for the rest of your damned life."

LARRY STRIPPED THE BED, tearing a corner of one sheet in his haste. He had satisfied a too-long suppressed lust at the expense of Theresa. No woman deserved to be used in that way. He hadn't felt so disgusted with himself since Patrick had found him passed out on that bench in the bus station. Only after debasing himself in front of Patrick and Gillian had he been able to see the fool he'd become. This episode with Theresa, likewise, gave him fresh perspective.

As he stuffed the sheets into the washing machine, the truth became clear. Patrick's church had died with him. It was gone.

An eerie quiet followed his acceptance. Larry stood still, his hands sunk into the wrinkled sheets. He saw himself tucking the tiny sailboat into the crook of Patrick's arm and closing the coffin lid. At that moment he had understood that they were burying more than a man. Why had he changed his mind within minutes and made his rash promise? He tried, again, to recapture the feelings of that moment but could only remember his boasting, empty words. Was it ego, stepping behind that lectern vacated by Reverend Pierce, stepping once again into the limelight? Or had he simply said what everyone wanted to hear, just as he always had when in front of an audience.

The Filigree Cross

He leaned against the washer, weight on his arms, and felt his soul crack. What could ever replace the inexplicable joy that performing had brought him before truth intervened?

ALL DAY HE SIFTED THROUGH the financial statements of the church. He concentrated on seeing the numbers, not the faces or the effort behind them. The church-held investments would meet its charitable obligations for many years. The mansion, his home and the administrative building would sell for many millions, extending that time. He felt sure that Sue and Fiona would agree that all the assets, beyond what they needed personally, should support the work of the church.

By five o'clock he felt almost ready to call Sue. Putting it off another few minutes, he wandered through his elegant rooms. What would he take with him when he left? Only his carvings and his books. They would no longer fit in a shopping bag and he would not get drunk and leave them on a bus, but he would leave carrying only what he had brought to the party. He would seek out a sheltered corner of the world where no one had ever heard of Larry Broadfellow, evangelist, where he could be a mere human. Relief, born, he knew, of simply giving up, gave him some peace.

The piercing jangle of the phone reminded him that he was a long way from freedom. He picked up the receiver to hear Mark shouting hysterically into his ear. "Turn on channel six. Quick. Jesus, Larry—" The line disconnected.

Marlene Baird

One of the country's most recognized news anchors read the monitor. Larry caught him in mid-sentence. ". . . substantiated by newspaper accounts."

Superimposed behind the reporter were two pictures. One was of a group of four children in front of the old church orphanage. The small head with the circle around it was his. He had never seen the picture before. Beside that was a picture of Patrick, one of the station's file photos.

"Coincidentally, less than two months ago, that same Larry Broadfellow, then the church's incredibly successful evangelist, made a dramatic departure wherein he cited God's having abandoned him. Was he being honest, or did he foresee this revelation?"

Larry reached for the phone and it rang in his hand. "Christ, Larry, I don't know what the hell is happening," Mark blurted. "That story did not come from me. You've got to believe me. I never told a single soul, I swear—"

"I missed the beginning. I assume they have the story of the charges against Patrick and his defection from Trinity Church?"

"Everything. Patrick *and* you. And they made it sound like a sordid movie."

"You didn't destroy those reports?"

"I threw them away."

"Where?"

"In the office."

Larry ignored the racing of his heart. "Was your office locked?"

"Yeah. I'm pretty sure." Larry heard Mark gulp. "To be honest, Larry, I was drinking. I'd just left the

The Filigree Cross

mansion after the ambulance took Fiona to the hospital. I hated everything about myself."

"We've never had trouble with the cleaning people. It's someone who had access to your office."

Mark continued to mumble apologies.

"Mark, stop. Think about who was there."

But Larry suddenly knew. 'I could have saved you,' she had said. Only Theresa and Tech would have had keys to Mark's office. Evidently she had held the information close for some time. This was what she had meant by her threat. This was what his crude behavior had brought down on them all.

Theresa was wrong on one count; Larry no longer wanted saving. But Patrick and Gillian—their exemplary lives could not be reduced to this. Their reputations had to be salvaged.

He barked instructions at Mark. "We answer no questions about the specific charges; don't dignify them with replies. Then we put into play the best damn PR job you can muster. We identify the church's dozens of perpetual charities—without dollar amounts. Then the scholarships, disaster relief assistance—"

Mark joined in. "Bible distributions, foreign missionary services. I got it."

"Get it all out there. I don't suppose anything will erase the dirty images that have been created in people's minds, but the public will have to judge for itself whether or not we've been a decent church. Remind everyone of the dedication of Patrick and Gillian. Leave me out of that part. If they want to go back in history so can we. Play up the poor beginnings. Maybe we can sabotage this train before it gets up too much steam."

"Who do you think—?"

"Doesn't matter. It's done. You've got plenty to do, and I have to call Hawaii."

"ALOHA," SUE SAID. Her voice almost hummed. "You sound happy."

"Larry! Mother and I are making Portuguese Sweet Bread. You should just smell this kitchen."

"I wish I could. Things over here are not so tranquil. I've got some terrible news." He heard an intake of breath and continued immediately. "The evening news just carried the story of the old child-abuse charges against Patrick."

Sue, obviously shocked into silence, could only murmur in disbelief as Larry told her the story of Mark's uncovering all of the material, and its being turned over to the broadcaster by someone as yet unidentified.

"Wait, Larry." He could almost see her holding up her hand to stop him. It must be almost too much to take in. She took several deep breaths. "Oh, this is so horrible. Is this going to finish the church for good?"

Larry answered obliquely, avoiding the real answer, that the church had already collapsed on his own shoulders. "I've got Mark started on an image campaign for the church, to protect the family's name."

"Do you think Grandpa would want that? Exposing all his good works for the sake of a media battle? But, of course, if there's any hope at all of bringing the church back, this needs to be put to rest. I guess you're right, Larry. A good offense is what we need."

The Filigree Cross

Now Larry was grasping for words. "Well, about that. Actually, I was going to call you just before all this broke. Sue, I can't do it. I can't put myself in Patrick's place. I'm simply not the man he was, not even close."

"But you don't even want to fight for it? You promised—"

"And I meant it, then. But it's not in me. You can't know how difficult it is to admit that."

An awful silence followed. "Sue?"

"You're absolutely sure about your decision?" she asked, her voice thick with disappointment.

"I wish it weren't true. I hate to make you unhappy."

"Then I don't want to go ahead with the public relations battle. I just know Grandpa would hate that. If the church has to die, let it go in peace. I have to hang up now."

IN THE FOLLOWING DAYS the newspapers treated the story with slightly more prudence than the first reporter had, but they could not resist tantalizing readers, merely sprinkling their reports with words like alleged and suspected. The most damning aspect seemed to be that Patrick had not fought the supposedly false accusations, but had turned tail. Thousands of letters arrived. The early ones expressed disbelief of the story and support for the church. Ultimately, however, hate surfaced. The numbers of disillusioned followers grew by the hour. Many even demanded the return of their contributions.

Mark, being the sole administrator left in the office, bore the brunt of the abuse. "Idiots!" he exclaimed over the phone to Larry. "Do they think all that money is sitting in a bank account somewhere just waiting to be sent back?"

"You sound beat. Will my coming down to the office be of any help?" Larry asked. It was a hollow offer; he wanted only to continue the packing of his few things in preparation for escape. Sue's clear disappointment in him had increased his desire to disappear.

"You'd only expose yourself to these damn photographers. Leeches. And have you seen that English web site? Jesus, they're calling us the 'Church of Man's Deceit.' You can find us on the net by searching for the word scam."

"Take it easy, Mark. It's horrible now, but the public will forget us before their Christmas bills are paid. I've talked to Sue and Fiona," he said. "They've agreed to the sale of the buildings. Our response to demands for money will be that all profits will go directly to the charities."

Mark's voice fell. "I just can't believe it," he muttered. "The millions who loved Patrick and you . . ."

"We had a great run. The church did a lot of good, and will continue to do so for some time."

"What will you do?"

Larry appreciated Mark's concern—he had his own future to worry about, without a personal fortune to fall back on. "I'm going abroad. I'm going to find a village without television, if such a thing exists. I picture goats on the dusty streets and barefoot children."

"Since you're on the Board, we'll need you from time to time, for signatures and such."

The Filigree Cross

"I'll get a post office box. But I only want to get mail that is crucial to winding down the church. It's cowardly, but I really don't want to see anything else."

"Forgive me if this sounds personal, Larry, but won't Sue and her mother need your support more than ever?"

"I'd be no good to them right now."

"Larry, I wish you great luck. You've been a good friend."

"I expect you'll be needed as an overseer for a long time yet, then there will be a generous severance. Enough to take good care of those kids."

"I won't forget what your giving me a second chance has meant."

"I'll let you know when I leave, and where I'll be."

Larry replaced the receiver and walked to the window. Dusk came early now. As the room darkened, Larry stood with his back to his carved birds, his constant, quiet friends, and gazed at the corner of the mansion. An anvil settled in his heart. Where was there a road that raised dust so thick he could hide in it?

CHAPTER THIRTY

EVERYONE WHO CARED now knew Larry's address—pictures of the mansion and his home had appeared in all major newspapers. When stacks of unwanted mail obliterated the surface of the cherrywood side table just inside his front door, he registered a change of address with the post office, forwarding everything to Mark. As he dumped the accumulated letters into a sack to take to the office, he noticed an envelope from the Salvation Army. They thanked him for his earlier offer to help serve dinners on Christmas Day. A bright red flyer, decorated in simple line drawings of holly, bore a map which showed him where he should be, and when.

Larry tossed it into the wastebasket. Though he had not been able to pinpoint a destination, he hoped to be away before Christmas, at least on the first leg to somewhere. Much as the idea of escape appealed to him, he could not actually visualize himself in some foreign place with dirt beneath his feet. But he needed only to look at the bundle of mail on the floor to remember that it was necessary to go; that this life would haunt him as long as he was within its reach.

The Filigree Cross

Two hours later, desolate in his isolation, he retrieved the flyer from the wastebasket. He had thwarted so many people's dreams lately. This simple act might redeem a minute part of him. Even that slim portion seemed important.

HUNGRY MEN AND families huddled, three-deep, in a line that extended for several city blocks. Larry moved to the front of the queue and squeezed himself through the doorway without incident. The difference between his clothing and that of the others shouted the fact that he was not there to commandeer anyone's meal.

The enormous hall sweated as outside drizzle rode in on soaked clothing. Vaporized in the sudden warmth, the moisture released smells that transported Larry back to his wasted years. Sweat and filth, added to constant anxiety, created a stench one could never forget. He maneuvered between rows of long tables jammed with bodies. Voices, raised to unusual exuberance, created a continuous roar.

He pushed through swinging doors to the kitchen. Boiling pots roiled steam into the air. It swirled with the heat from open oven doors and massive stovetops. The result was air almost too heavy to breath. Immediately a man approached—maybe forty years old, his T-shirt damp-stuck to a thin torso. His face portrayed controlled panic.

"I'm Jason. We need a gravy maker. Drop your coat in the vestibule." He pointed, and Larry moved to an alcove where more than two dozen coats lay on a table. There were ripped jackets and fur coats and slick trench coats in the pile.

Jason directed Larry between hustling bodies, too busy to look up in greeting, and deposited him in front of a pan that covered all of the burners on the stove. "You a cook?" he asked.

"Never tried it."

"Welcome to one of the finest Epicurean schools in the country." Jason grinned and stuck out his hand, waiting for a name.

"Larry. Glad to meet you, Jason."

In the pan lay three inches of bubbling fat and juices. Jason handed him a quart-sized plastic container. "Fill this about half full with cold water. Add flour and mix until you have a light paste." His quick eyes connected with Larry's. "Are you with me?"

"Paste I can recognize."

"When it's well blended, pour it slowly into the fat and stir. Whatever you do, keep stirring." He picked up a long-handled slotted spoon and ran it thoroughly through the liquid. "Like so. If you don't keep it moving, you'll end up with lumps, and, even though our clientele is not usually fussy, we pride ourselves on no lumps."

Jason bumped Larry on the arm with his fist. "Good luck." He engaged Larry's eyes again. "You a celebrity?" he asked. "You look familiar."

Larry laughed. "Hardly."

Someone across the thirty-foot kitchen yelled for Jason.

Larry swiped at sweat on his hairline with the back of his arm, smiling. All he had to do was avoid lumps. If he could accomplish that, it would be the most constructive thing he'd done in a long time.

The Filigree Cross

Four hours later he was slicing turkey breast like a pro—a perfect edge of brown skin on each piece. His socks were soaked, his fancy loafers wet and coated with grease. Volunteers came and retreated as shifts changed. Only Jason and the smell of dinner and the noise were constant.

"You need a break?" Jason asked late in the afternoon.

Larry shook his head. "I've needed this like you can never guess."

Jason smiled. "Oh, I can guess," he said.

In the kitchen one could almost forget the reason for all the labor, but once out in the large hall, where Larry occasionally refilled coffee cups or milk glasses and wiped tables, every face reminded him.

A bearded man, hunched inside a green plaid jacket, complained about the potatoes. "Not done," he muttered, scooping them quickly between rows of dark teeth. A young girl sat on his right. Larry, carrying a heavy coffee jug and passing down the table on the opposite side, saw gentle blue eyes wrinkle in a shy smile as she said, "Mine are terrific."

Immediately her mother snatched at her arm and jerked her around. "Ruth-Anne! Don't talk to him!"

The girl's slight frame spun around with the force of her mother's grip. Bright red spots of embarrassment rose on the girl's pale skin. She tried to concentrate on her own dinner as her mother scolded her harshly with repeated warnings. Larry felt sorry for the girl who glanced side-to-side, embarrassed at the attention her mother's ravings were attracting. But, then, how could he judge this woman? What did he know of these lives? Maybe that shrill lecture would save the little girl from harm one day.

At eight-thirty in the evening the line finally dwindled and Jason locked the doors. While the last hundred or so of the hungry finished their meals, Larry sat on a wooden bench in the back of the hall where it was cool, while yet another volunteer crew cleaned the kitchen.

Larry examined his pink, wrinkled hands. He rubbed out a sore spot in the palm of his right hand, then switched the massage to his lower back.

Jason plunked down beside him. "If you're not used to this, everything will ache tomorrow," he said.

"Well, then, I'm in for a load of pain. But right now I feel terrific. Never knew it could hurt this good. How long have you been helping out?"

Jason rubbed his forehead with one hand and ripe body odor mingled with Larry's own. "Five years next month. Enjoyed many a meal here before I graduated."

"Graduated?" Larry asked.

"From the U of AA," he said. "Now I volunteer for two meals every week and, of course, we're all needed on holidays."

Jason leaned forward, his hands on his knees and looked into Larry's face. "I remembered where I've seen you. You're Larry Broadfellow. What's the story?"

Larry shook his head. "It's all a mistake, but negatives can't always be proven."

Jason rose stiffly and stuck out his hand. "Well, don't let them run you off. We had several compliments on the gravy."

The Filigree Cross

EVEN AFTER SHOWERING AT LENGTH Larry could smell turkey grease on his skin. At midnight he wandered his bedroom. In the silk brocade of his comforter, in the polished grain of his bureau, he saw images. The faces of the day had registered despair, disbelief, fear. The bodies beneath the faces were curled into the posture of capitulation—walking and sitting bent, glancing covertly. Only the children had looked straight into his face; only their faces still wore some hope. Where would Ruth-Ann and the mother, who was near to breaking, sleep tonight? Knowing they might be in a damp room, or the back seat of a cold car, or worse, he couldn't get into his huge bed.

He woke with the winter sun bleeding into the den. He rose slowly from the sofa, his back and shoulders objecting, every strained muscle reminding him of his lazy life. He stuck his feet into slippers and sat draped in soft blankets against the chill. Of the thousands he had seen yesterday, only Jason recognized him. He wouldn't have to go to the ends of the earth to disappear. Anonymity was assured among this subculture to whom a flamboyant personality like Larry Broadfellow was as remote as safety.

CHAPTER THIRTY-ONE

"THANK GOODNESS I FINALLY got you," Larry said when a man answered the phone. It had taken him two days to reach Jason. He had not been at the Salvation Army hall when Larry sought him out and, earlier, had not answered the phone at the number Larry had been given.

"Who is this?"

"Oh, Jason, it's Larry Broadfellow. I've been trying to get in touch with you.

"You sound stressed. What's the problem?"

"Insomnia, to be honest. But I've been thinking about a young girl and her mother who were at the Christmas dinner. The little girl's name is Ruth-Anne, I don't know her mother's name."

"That would be Joanne Mitchell. A tough situation."

"Can you give me any details?"

Jason told him that at age twenty-seven Joanne had borne her first child after twelve years of prostitution and addiction.

"Have you known her that long?"

The Filigree Cross

"We shared a few bottles of wine in our time, when we happened to be at the same place at the same time. She was just one of the girls. But she tried real hard to stay off the stuff when she got pregnant, and Ruth-Anne seems relatively healthy."

"I'd like to help them."

Larry was surprised at the long pause before Jason spoke. "Do you see yourself handing them money?" he asked.

"Maybe."

"Joanne would blow it in a minute. The more you gave her the faster she'd get rid of it. Besides, she would have every doper she'd ever met hanging on her. It wouldn't even be safe."

"What about a new environment?"

"Larry, I know your heart is in the right place, but it's not that easy. You can't take a woman who has spent her entire adult life on the street and stick her in suburbia."

"Is there any way to separate Ruth-Anne from her mother?"

"I don't know that she's in any immediate danger by social services standards. Besides, if you're not family, it takes an act of Congress. Parental ties are hard to break, legally and emotionally. The little girl wouldn't thank you."

"Do you know where they live?"

Jason sighed, showing his impatience. "The last I knew was Mason Arms. Low-income housing that's become a series of flop-houses. But I don't recommend a personal contact. These people are unbelievably defensive. Your best intentions can cause a lot of pain. That's why organizations like the Army do a better job. We give them some distance, allow them some degree of dignity."

"I'll keep that in mind. And I'll be down at the hall to help serve the weekend meals."

LARRY PARKED THE LINCOLN six blocks away from Mason Arms and even at that was prepared to come back to a stripped car. Most of the snow was gone but a brisk wind kept his coat flapping as he walked. There were three apartment buildings in the complex, each four stories high. Paper bags and plastic cups and used prophylactics sifted over the mushy ground and piled up against the chain-link fence. The sidewalks had crumbled in many places and cement chunks were scattered throughout the yard, as if thrown by children. Larry walked slowly toward the first building until he was stopped cold by a memory. He rocked to a stop, his head swimming for a moment. On a decent stretch of sidewalk a child had drawn connecting square boxes with chalk and numbered them one to eight. A half moon finished one end of the drawing. Hopscotch. He had last seen the game played in the orphanage at Madison. Those were the days when, as a youngster, he waited for letters from the Brannigans. The memory brought a rush of the old anxiety, and the skin on his arms pricked. He shrugged it off, shook his head and stepped around the drawing.

In the lobby of the building were a series of in-wall mailboxes, the names having been crossed out so many times most of them were unreadable.

"Who you lookin' for?"

Larry turned, startled. He had seen no one and heard no one approach. The man was middle-aged,

The Filigree Cross

dressed warmly in well-used clothes. He stared at Larry's shoes, his coat, and finally his face. Larry had thought to exchange his luxurious topcoat for a raincoat and his loafers for tennis shoes, but he had nothing in his closet that would allow him to fit in here.

"Do you know Joanne Mitchell?" he asked.

The flash in the green eyes told Larry that the man did know her. He looked away from Larry and chewed on his lip. "Would she want to see you?" he asked, turning back.

"I'm a friend," Larry said.

The man's eyebrows rose. "Jake won't like that."

So she had a boyfriend. That would complicate matters.

"It's not what you're thinking. We're old friends."

The man grunted. "There's no such thing." He seemed to have become bored with the conversation and walked off. "Third floor, east end," he mumbled, his back to Larry as he went outside.

Dirt sloped like drifted snow at the edges of the stairs and the carpet lay in strips that could trip you. The smell told Larry that the plumbing had failed in more than one apartment. He climbed, shaking his head. The three hundred thousand he had offered to Tech, which had seemed like an immaterial amount of money, might restore all three buildings to something in which a person could take some pride. He remembered what Tech had said—they weren't dollars, they were just numbers. The church had been generous, supporting many charities, but not once had Larry made an attempt to actually see what was being done. Had he been too busy, or too insensitive, to look into the faces of the needy?

Larry stood at the door at the east end of the hall and could not knock. Who did he think he was, coming to spy on these lives now, after so many years of neglect?

The door swung open and he was nearly bowled over by a man in a hurry. "What the hell?" the man shouted as they both regained their balance.

He assessed Larry with quick, dark eyes, then laughed, showing white teeth. He shouted back into the apartment. "Joanne, come see. Santa finally came."

Joanne Mitchell appeared in the doorway, looking calmer and prettier than she had at the dinner. Perhaps she was not completely sober. She smiled at Jake and took in Larry. "Santa?"

"I recognize the get-up," Jake said. "He's one of those do-gooders."

Joanne straightened and stopped smiling. "From social services?"

Larry answered. "No."

"Who the hell are you, then?" Jake asked, putting his face right up to Larry's. He was tall and wiry, maybe forty years old. And maybe me, Larry thought, if Fiona hadn't almost hit me with the Oldsmobile as I staggered down that road.

Larry pulled himself up, searching for the right words. "I was a volunteer—"

"Told you," Jake said.

Larry addressed Joanne. "I was a volunteer at the Salvation Army Christmas dinner and saw you and your daughter there. I wondered if I could be of help."

The Filigree Cross

Jake poked Larry, hard, in the chest. "I take care of this family." Larry stuck his hands in the pockets of his raincoat so as not to appear confrontational. Jake poked again, harder, so that Larry stepped back a few inches. Larry looked at Joanne. Her face was immobile. Her expressionless eyes moved over to Jake. She backed into the apartment and closed the door.

"Where's Ruth-Anne?" Larry asked.

"None of your damn business, but she's at school. Now get the hell out of my sight." Jake cocked his head toward the apartment door. "She doesn't want your help and neither do I."

Larry left the complex and walked the six blocks to his car in a trance. He felt like an alien, as though he had grown ragged wings and talons and was circling with intent to harm. Or some futuristic big-headed man whose intellect was vastly more powerful than his puny body. To these people, he *was* that weird, and they would never trust him.

He didn't know these people any better than he knew those in his audiences. In the early days, in the wooden hall when he first began to preach, he connected with them, knew them to some degree. He saw what they wore, how they stood, what their eyes had to say. But success had taken him behind the spotlight where he was, literally, blinded. Other than a few personal contacts he'd had, such as with Johnny Cameron and his grandmother, he couldn't remember one thing about any of the millions to whom he had preached. And, up until recently, it had not occurred to him that it mattered.

The Lincoln was intact. Someone had scratched lewd suggestions on the hood and fenders. Apparently

Marlene Baird

the large carpenter's nail which lay on the road had been the weapon. Larry had to smile. The writer had done no real harm, only reminded him that he was out of his depth. The car would still run, still take him where he needed to go. He pulled out his keys and with two smooth strokes scratched the Christian fish symbol on the driver's door.

The Filigree Cross

PART FOUR

1999

Redemption

Marlene Baird

CHAPTER THIRTY-TWO

AS SUE CAME IN WITH THE MAIL, Fiona turned from the kitchen counter where she had been drying lunchtime dishes. Again, Fiona marveled at her daughter's metamorphosis. Sue now walked with a loose gait, setting her muu-muu swinging, as if the sun, while bronzing her skin and veining her long brown hair with gold, had extracted all tension from her joints. In the four months on the Big Island, freed from her executive responsibilities, Sue had bloomed as fully as the lehua blossom lei she always wore. Today's was red, reminding Fiona of bottlebrush.

"Anything?" Fiona asked, glancing at the half dozen envelopes in Sue's hand.

"Nothing. And the wedding just a week away."

Fiona placed a bowl in the cupboard. "Not a word since his Christmas card. Surely he wouldn't miss your day for less than a compelling reason. You don't suppose he's ill?"

"I talked to Mark just yesterday," Sue replied. "He said Larry seems fine."

"I wish Mark would at least tell us where he is."

"Obviously Larry needs a break from the Brannigan family. He has belonged to us most of his life. I can't blame him for striking off on his own."

Fiona folded the dish towel and hung it over the handle of the oven. "I know. For a while I was afraid that looking out for me would bind him to the family again. But perhaps he'll surprise us and come to the wedding unannounced."

"Don't get your hopes up, Mother. That doesn't seem like something Larry would do."

As Sue sat down at the table to deal with the mail, Fiona drifted outside to the veranda. Its wooden floor, always moist, gave bounce to the lightest step. It spread forty feet across the front of the white bungalow, supported by pillars. The spacious old house with shuttered windows—no glass and no screens—had belonged to an aunt of Jimmy's, and before that, to his grandparents. Unruly grass spread over the large yard. The fence sagged from the weight of thick bougainvillea, dripping with blossoms. Many a day rain sheeted thickly from the sharply sloping roof to dig a horizontal line in the lawn just beyond the overhang. This afternoon, however, sunlight struck the pillars, the lips of the steps, every blade and leaf in the yard, with a metallic sharpness.

Fiona turned over the cushion of a worn wicker chair and settled onto its drier side. How silly of her to expect Larry to show up and surprise them. Would she never stop thinking like a foolish girl?

Lifting her long, cotton skirt to above her knees, she stretched her legs out to rest her ankles on an adjacent chair. Two boys, four and five, lived in the house next door and they were playing behind an

The Filigree Cross

unpainted wooden fence. Fiona couldn't understand the heavy pidgin slang they shouted to one another, but their giggles floated to her, and the smack of their hands on a ball. Then she heard the squeak of a screen door and their mother's voice calling them inside.

Eyes closed in the sudden quiet, Fiona tried to give herself over to the languid air and the desultory drone of nectar-laden insects, but found herself picturing Larry alone in some foreign place. She wished, again, she could take back the note she had written just after her arrival in Hawaii. She must have said something that had hurt or angered Larry because his return letter might have come from a stranger. He had responded to her as if they'd never kissed, never expressed their love. The exact words she had written escaped her memory, but no doubt the note had been lightly drafted and quickly mailed, with a child's forethought.

The squish of tires on rough asphalt made her turn toward the driveway. Jimmy bounded up the few stairs and kissed her cheek, as always. "How you doin', Mom?" It was his favorite way of teasing her, because, though she would very soon be his mother-in-law, they were only a few years apart in age. His language had reverted, charmingly, to the patois of the islands. It suited his evident comfort in being home. His frayed and wrinkled cut-offs showed strong, brown legs.

"Did you have a good morning?" Fiona asked.

"Super. I think everyone on the boat caught something. Lots of souvenir pictures." He struck a pose, holding his hand high, as if lifting a sporting fish, and grinned. "Haoli Heaven."

"I beg your pardon? Making fun of us?" Sue admonished from the doorway.

Marlene Baird

"Ah, my favorite invader." He kissed Sue and put an arm around her shoulders.

Flushing with pleasure, Sue told Fiona she and Jimmy were going to check on the new carpet for the Sunday School, then they had to pick up one of Jimmy's brothers at the airport in Hilo. "Shall we come back to get you for dinner?"

Fiona shook her head. "You two have a private evening for a change. I'm fine."

Fiona watched Sue and Jimmy drive off without a wave—laughing, sharing some secret, already absorbed in one another. As the truck disappeared around a corner, loneliness wrapped her. After the wedding, while Sue and Jimmy were on their honeymoon, she would scrub up the house and do some touch-up painting. She had ordered polished cotton slip-covers that Sue liked, and fresh rugs. When they returned the house would be full of flowers, and Fiona would be living in a small apartment she had found.

Fiona rose from her chair and began to hike along the ragged edge of the road. Between the straps of her sandals, grass licked at her toes. Her damp skirt clung to her legs and lethargy filled her whole being. Daydreaming about Larry, she felt an urgency rise through her body and she became aware of the pressure of her blouse across her breasts. She loosened her hair from its tie and shook it free. "Come back," she murmured.

AN HOUR LATER SHE RETURNED to the house, her skirt damp to the knees. Her blouse had pulled free from the waistband and her hair had frizzed

The Filigree Cross

into a bush from the humidity. She climbed the few steps to the veranda swinging her sandals in one hand.

The door stood open. As she stepped silently over the sill, her entire body contracted. The shadows of the room, dark after the outside sun, could not be read, but she smelled his cologne, and her heart hammered in her ears.

"Larry?" she whispered, leaning into the room.

She heard an intake of breath, then his voice, low and tight. "Against the sun you look like a wood nymph come to delight me."

Larry stepped forward. The half light showed a sharpened jaw; he had lost some weight. A glint from his belt buckle took her eye, then the drape of his shirt on his shoulders. Something new lighted his eyes. She wanted to leap at him, throw herself against him, but she held back. He came close, not touching her. His breath mingled with hers. So slowly she thought she would break, he brought one hand to her hair. The cords in his neck strained as he spoke. "Oh, I've missed this face."

Her eyes burned in their sockets as she studied him.

"Say you've missed me, at least a little," he said.

"You can't imagine."

His body tilted, maybe an inch closer.

The shoes dropped from her hand. "Tell me you've not just come for the wedding. Tell me you've come to stay."

"If you'll have me. I'm terribly poor, a pauper in fact."

His lips crushed hers to the point of bruising. The pain heightened her need. Her body folded into his, every surface straining for nearness. "I love you, I love you," she told him between kisses. Larry lifted her easily, carrying her down the hallway.

"Why did you come back to me now?" she whispered against his chest.

Larry stopped walking. "I came to believe that I deserved happiness. Then I talked to Sue, to be sure that I would not be interrupting your new life."

"She knew that I had no life without you."

As they entered Fiona's room the white walls and furniture were striped golden, cross-hatched by the sun filtering between the shutters. Fiona studied Larry's face as he moved toward the bed. His features rippled through the strips of light like those of a painted warrior. A chill spread through her. She shook her head to clear an image of another face, its ugliness pebbled by spots of sun shining through foliage. Don't be foolish, this is Larry, she told herself, but she smelled dry pine needles and felt small rocks on her back. She tensed against the muscles in Larry's arms, which pressed into her just as the other man's had.

Larry stopped at the edge of the bed, still holding her. She felt his body tighten. His eyes pinched closed and he shuddered. Then he settled her, tenderly, as if she were a baby, against soft pillows. He drew his thumb over the light scar above her eye, and backed away. "I'm sorry. I know what you must be remembering."

"No, no," she whispered, pulling him down to her. "Take me beyond this, Larry. You must."

HOURS LATER THEY WALKED the frothy beach. The moon, almost smothered behind a ragged

The Filigree Cross

cloud curtain, lent little illumination. When it receded completely, and pure blackness wrapped them, only their touching hands assured Fiona of Larry's presence. She grasped more tightly and leaned into him. There was no need to express her fullness, and words could not have captured it. She thought of the silent, breathless moments, then the explosive times when all the world, but the two of them, was reduced to skittering flashes of light.

They walked for a long time while she searched for her normal voice. It seemed important to come back to earth, to ground this miracle.

"Since you never went to the ends of the earth, where I've been picturing you, I guess you've been emptying the mansion and getting it ready for sale."

"Everything is in storage waiting for you and Sue to make the final decisions. She said she didn't want to take it on just before the wedding."

"Before I left Chicago I tried to find something special of Mother's. Did you happen to come across a piece of jewelry, a very fine gold cross? As a young teenager I used to ask to wear it, but she refused to let me. She would only say that, perhaps, and the accent was on the 'perhaps,' one day it would be mine."

He was so quiet the brush of the tide sounded loud in her ears. "Larry?" she said, tugging at him.

"I have the cross," he said slowly. "She left it to me."

There was such sadness in his voice Fiona stopped walking. "You? Why did she give it to you?"

Once again he lapsed into silence. Fiona realized they were near one of her favorite resting places. She led him to an eroded rowboat, turned upside down. "Let's sit."

Larry tested its frame for his weight, then sat.

"Don't you want to talk about this?" she asked.

"It's not that. It would be good to talk about it, especially with you."

He shifted just slightly away from her so that they weren't touching. "Gillian wrote me a letter that I could not read until after her death. The cross was inside the envelope, folded in half. It had become a symbol to her. Jesus' cross, so frail that she could bend it. That reminded her of me. You see, many years ago, long before I began to doubt myself, she saw the emptiness within me."

Fiona put her hand on his arm.

"I've often wondered why she didn't approach me sooner, but I realize now that she was concerned about the church. She would never have done anything to damage your father's church, for it was his whole life." Larry put his arm around her and she moved closer to him. "Would you like to have the cross?" he asked. "I'll have it repaired."

"I want you to tell me that it no longer represents you."

He kissed her forehead. "I treasure it, because it was given with such courage and love. But I don't need it anymore. I've found my core. I'm steady, and sure of God's place in my life. I think Gillian would be very happy to know that."

"What changed you?"

He paused for a moment. "Do you know, until a few months ago I'd never so much as prepared a meal?"

The Filigree Cross

Fiona chuckled. "Me neither. Sue says I'm making progress though. I'll cook for you. But what happened, did Gloria go on strike?"

"I helped prepare and serve dinners at the Salvation Army at Christmas."

"I remember your promising to do that."

"There was one little girl there whom I can't forget. Ruth-Anne Mitchell, probably because she's about the age I was when I was orphaned. After I left that building that evening, my own home seemed unreal. The price of my dining room table would have fed the two of them for years. I wanted so badly to help them but I didn't know how to go about it. But I was committed to helping change lives like theirs." He paused. "When I told you I was poor, I wasn't kidding. I've used all of my investments to set up a foundation called Gillian's Hope. It will be staffed by professionals and provide housing and transportation and child care for those families who have a chance to become self-sufficient."

"For how many, and for how long? Did you have a great fortune?"

"I had a lot more than I'd realized, and a thousand times more than anyone could ever need. I'll find a way to earn more, to keep the foundation going, but it will mean going back to the mainland. Will you miss this paradise?"

"There are other paradises," Fiona said, lifting his hand to her lips.

LARRY SWEATED BESIDE JIMMY and a team of men, raising one wall of the new church. He glanced, hopefully, upwards. Every half hour there had been a spit of rain to cool them and he was more than ready for the next one.

He and Jimmy put their shoulders to the frame and the skeleton wall rose steadily, meeting the already standing adjacent one. Half of the team held it firmly in place while the others placed joining brackets.

When they were able to step away, Larry grabbed a water bottle and wandered toward the existing church which crouched small beside the new structure. It had been recently repainted white, and now, rain-washed, glistened against the rich grass. He followed a crushed coral path, deep pink from moisture.

He heard Jimmy's steps behind him, then his voice. "Half of this will become a meeting room, the other half, the Sunday School. Sue has every kid in town in love with her because she let them vote on the carpet color. It's the first time I've ever seen her with children and she's a natural."

Larry opened the door and had to dip his head to clear the casing. He peered down the narrow aisle that separated a dozen rows of pews. The windows were shuttered against the rain, so the only light—a suffused glow—came through a simple stained-glass window at the far end, above the pulpit. He stepped inside. Now rain pattered on the metallic roof and rustled in the greenery outside. He sat gingerly on the edge of a pew. His eyes closed and his head fell forward, releasing all the strain in his back. "Thank you, Lord, for bringing me to such happiness," he murmured.

When he stepped back outside Jimmy was waiting.

"Sue and I have been wondering if you would address the congregation one day."

The Filigree Cross

Larry shook his head. "Thank you, that's very kind. But I'm finished with being up front. I'll be in my seat on Sunday, and every Sunday thereafter."

AS LARRY PASSED through the lobby of his hotel, the desk clerk hailed him and handed him a fat manila envelope. After his shower Larry ripped it open—another batch of papers regarding the sale of the mansion. A sheet of paper, clipped to a smaller envelope, bore Mark's writing. "I know you didn't want any personal stuff, but I think you should see this."

Larry opened the letter hesitantly, but then was glad Mark had sent it. It was from Johnny Cameron. His studies were going well.

I know I'm on the right track, thanks to you, Mr. Broadfellow, but I have sad news. My Gram passed away two months ago. I guess you didn't get my letter.

I am so glad that I made the decision to enter the ministry while she was alive. I think it was one of the happiest days of her life when you offered me this chance and I took it. We will never forget you. I've heard all the awful news stories and don't believe any of them. I hope you will never forget all of us whose lives you have changed. I don't know if you are going to preach again—I hope so. I know Gram would like to hear you.

Take care of yourself, Johnny Cameron.

P.S. Maybe you'll have time to write me some time.

Larry's head dropped. Johnny had written after his grandmother's death, when he needed support. Even if Mark had seen the letter, which would have arrived when Larry was still floundering, he had only followed Larry's instructions by not forwarding it.

'Gram would like to hear you.' The young man was still thinking, first, about his grandmother even though she was far beyond any mortal suffering.

Larry picked up his phone and dialed Jimmy. "I would like an opportunity to speak on Sunday if it can be arranged. Just a few words."

Jimmy's voice revealed his anticipation. "I'll get in touch with Reverend Akala right away."

"Only a couple of words. Nothing major."

"Whatever you want, Larry."

IT DID NOT RAIN FOR THREE DAYS and Sunday brought blistering sunlight and heat. Larry was grateful for the shadowy corner behind the choir where he stood awaiting his introduction. Sweating believers streamed across the worn floors of the modest church. Soon, the narrow passageways along the sides of the room were filled with people standing, blocking out most of the window light, and more jammed themselves into the few feet between the last pew and the door.

Pastor Akala stepped to the pulpit. Barely into his thirties, he had been in their community only six months, following the passing of their former minister. When they had met during the week, Larry found him earnest, though nervous about leading his first church.

The Filigree Cross

The pastor cleared his throat, and people stopped fanning their faces with the day's program. In an unpracticed voice he began. "I wish we had our new, larger church today," he said. "So many of us have come to hear a special visitor." He paused for a moment, head bent, then continued. "I'll forgo our usual program. After our prayer and the first hymn I will relinquish this space to Mr. Larry Broadfellow, a man I've met recently. Many of you know of his television broadcasts. I had seen one or two of them, and I'm sure you will find as I did, that the real Larry Broadfellow is not what one might expect."

Larry chose to accept that as a compliment. It had been clear at their meeting that Reverend Akala, with the unfettered skepticism of youth, was not a fan of any televangelists.

After the opening prayer, Jimmy motioned to the organist who played the introduction to the hymn. More than two hundred voices joined him, their voices swirling in the tight space and pouring out into the neighborhood.

As the hymn ended and Larry moved forward, he felt the old surge rising up through his legs. He slowed his step. No more of that. Just a simple prayer for Johnny and his grandmother. But the tingle spread to his fingertips. He jammed both hands in his jacket pockets and aligned himself directly behind the pulpit. He lowered his head and began a prayer, one of Patrick's favorites. "The Lord is here with us today," he began. "I know, because I brought Him with me, and you did, too. And wherever men gather in His glory we bathe in His love."

Quiet Amens drifted up to him. His arms twitched, so he brought his hands to grip the splintered wooden podium. He felt electrically charged, as if he would burst unless he moved. Fighting it, he continued. "We bathe in His love. Let it embrace you. Let it sustain you. Breathe it in . . . the world's only perfect love." He drew in a deep breath. When he released it, in a noisy rush of air, a spasm gripped his shoulders and he could no longer be still. He stepped out from behind the podium and began to move, pacing the short distance available to him. He felt awkward and sensed discomfort in the congregation.

He tried to smile encouragingly. "I had no idea this was going to be difficult. Talking quietly, I mean." A few took his meaning and laughed softly. Struggling for a beginning, he stopped abruptly, raised his arms to the ceiling, and whispered. "Here I am, God. Here I am. Do what you will."

As he brought his arms down, thoughts formed. "There is a young man in seminary school who wrote to tell me that his grandmother had passed away. I knew the family only briefly, but enough to realize that she was a woman of unusual faith. Johnny Cameron was probably seventeen when I first met him at a live service. When I asked him, before the camera, what he would have God grant him, he answered that he wanted his grandmother to be able to leave her wheelchair." Larry moved to the opposite side of the small stage. "In all the world, this teenager wanted only for his grandmother to walk without pain."

He let his gaze encompass the entire room. "These two people were totally devoted to one another, their

The Filigree Cross

lives stuffed full of common caring. They exemplified God's best."

Larry moved back behind the pulpit. "Well, Maureen Cameron is walking with God, without pain, today, and I hope she can hear me. I want to thank her for raising such a marvelous boy."

Larry hesitated, feeling a catch in his voice. Almost to himself, he said, "Johnny's letter brought me back here, to the pulpit. And now I know that this is where I belong." Tears stung as Patrick's face came before him. How Patrick would have loved to hear him say that.

He sought out the faces of Fiona and Sue. Fiona sat, fingers pressed to her mouth, her eyes large. He couldn't read her expression. Sue grinned and drew her fingers out as though along a string—their signal, during tapings and live broadcasts, to keep going.

Larry cleared the heavy emotion from his voice. He glanced at Pastor Akala, relaxing in his chair. He smiled at Larry and seemed in no hurry to take control.

Larry gripped the wooden surface, shaking the podium slightly. "This is where the Lord intended for me to be." His voice began to rise as his body filled with energy. "Undeserving, I was given a talent. Unwittingly, I used it without true purpose. But I now accept my gift and pledge to use it only in the pure worship of God." He felt the concentration of the congregation as they tried to grasp his meaning, for he had moved to a purely personal revelation. But even their silence was infused with a vigor which seemed to bleed upward into his own body, as though they urged him along. Once again, he corralled his impulse to strut, though every sinew in his legs ached.

Marlene Baird

"A few months ago I was beaten. The news media disgraced me and those I love. Thousands who had showered me with adoration shunned me. But all of that was nothing compared to what I did to myself. I succumbed to self-pity. I abandoned my principles and reneged on my promises. I turned away from obligations, eager to be free of any commitments."

Larry's body began to move in rhythm with the words. He unbuttoned his jacket and reached out over the audience. Every face shifted toward him.

"I became self-centered and deserved to be lost in the wilderness." He paused, then placed both hands on his chest. "But God, He saw something salvageable." Larry dropped his voice and enunciated each word. "God sent me to volunteer at a soup kitchen, and taught me how to feed myself. I was starved. I had never learned how to partake of God's bounty." Holding his hand in the air like an eager child in a classroom, he asked, "Have you learned how the Lord feeds us? Show me your hands." A few arms rose slightly, then fell back into laps.

"It's a tough question, isn't it? God's blessings had lain all around me, flowed over me. I had the caring of loved ones, good health, the ability to make a living. But I took them as my own." He raised both arms above his head, his jacket flying open. "By denying that these blessing came from God, *I* was taking the credit." He saw heads nodding. He punched the air with a fist. "That's why I toppled. Not because of what the outside world was doing to me but because, inside, I was alone and therefore weak."

Several people clapped, and someone shouted, "Amen, brother," and he was transported. These two

The Filigree Cross

hundred people became two thousand, twenty thousand, a hundred and twenty thousand. He needed to tell them all.

But this was not his day, this was only his baptism.

He collected himself, rebuttoning his jacket with fingers that resisted. He looked to Reverend Akala. "Thank you for this opportunity to speak. You will never know what it has meant to me."

As he returned to his corner behind the choir, the congregation rose to their feet and Jimmy led them in another hymn. Untrained voices strained at the high notes as these humble people sang to a simpler God than Larry had previously known. Was it was easier to feel close to God in a place where the wind always bore the scent of flowers? If so, that only meant that he was needed more on the harsh streets of Chicago.

Larry's eyes were drawn to the stained-glass window above his head. Air-borne dust motes reflected the window's jewel tones and the swirling mass of color resembled a tumbling sea. Larry's face cracked in a smile. "Patrick, dear friend," he whispered, "I'm tacking into the wind, but I'm on course."

About the Author

Marlene Baird writes diverse novels, the common thread being that dramatic experiences cause her characters to examine their lives. Three of her short stories have been published, and she has won numerous honors in nationwide writing contests.

A transplanted Canadian, Marlene became an American citizen in June 2001 and lives in Arizona with her husband Bob. She served on the board of Professional Writers of Prescott for three years and is a member of the Arizona Authors Association. *The Filigree Cross* is her second published work, the first being a mystery titled *Murder Times Two*.

Printed in the United States
909000001B